How to Talk Dirty

Transform Your Sex Life & Spike Up Your Libido. 200 Real Dirty Talk Tips to Drive Your Partner Wild. Make Your Partner Your "Sex Slave"

© **Copyright 2019 by Eva Harmon - All rights reserved.**

The content contained within this book may not be reproduced, duplicated or transmitted without direct written permission from the author or the publisher.

Under no circumstances will any blame or legal responsibility be held against the publisher, or author, for any damages, reparation, or monetary loss due to the information contained within this book. Either directly or indirectly.

Legal Notice:

This book is copyright protected. This book is only for personal use. You cannot amend, distribute, sell, use, quote or paraphrase any part, or the content within this book, without the consent of the author or publisher.

Disclaimer Notice:

Please note the information contained within this document is for educational and entertainment purposes only. All effort has been executed to present accurate, up to date, and reliable, complete information. No warranties of any kind are declared or implied. Readers acknowledge that the author is not engaging in the rendering of legal, financial, medical or professional advice. The content within this book has been derived from various sources. Please consult a licensed professional before attempting any techniques outlined in this book.

By reading this document, the reader agrees that under no circumstances is the author responsible for any losses, direct or indirect, which are incurred as a result of the use of information contained within this document, including, but not limited to, — errors, omissions, or inaccuracies.

Table of Contents

Introduction.................................5

Chapter 1: Introducing Dirty Talk................................8

Chapter 2: Dirty Talk as Foreplay........................29

Chapter 3: Dirty Talk for Men...............................55

Chapter 4: Dirty Talk for Women........................75

Chapter 5: Digital Dirty Talk...............................92

Chapter 6: What NOT to Do..............................110

Chapter 7: Bonus Tips to Spice Up the Bedroom..........................125

Conclusion................................135

Introduction

Dirty talk: It is something that too many people feel awkward about. So many people find that even talking about sex in a normal way is just too much. There are people that are embarrassed to talk about what they want or how they feel. They are embarrassed to use words to describe what they enjoy or what they dislike, and unfortunately, that embarrassment of talking about what is wanted is linked to a lack of intimacy as well.

What makes sex good? For some people, it is intimacy. For others, it is the raw, unadulterated passion. For others still, however, it is the simple act of communication. It is the communicating of what you want in bed; it is the idea that you can tell someone else precisely what it is that you want so that you can get it. If you want mind-blowing sex, then you need to know how to tell people what you want, and until you can do that, you will never have sex that is as good as you would like it to be.

There is an easy answer to being able to manage your sex life and make sure that you are getting that mind-blowing finale that you have been wanting. You can learn to make your partner want you more than ever just by learning how to communicate better in ways that are both erotic and informative at the same time. The answer is with dirty talk.

Dirty talk is talking about the acts that you would like to do with your partner in a way that is arousing. It does not need to be demeaning or violent—but it certainly can be if both partners are in agreement. For some, being called a slut in the context of dirty talk can be highly arousing—it can elevate the experience that is being had. For others, that is not okay. It is important for you to understand what it is that you can and cannot say to someone else to keep them hot and bothered, and this book will be your guide.

As you read, you are going to learn all about how you can introduce dirty talk into your bedroom. You will learn how you can drive your partner *wild* for you with just a few simple words and learning to understand what it is that they want to hear. We are going to be going through what dirty talk is and how it serves as a sort of foreplay for your relationship. We will go over dirty talk for both men and women, as well as a guide to sexting and digitally talking dirty to your partner. We will consider what *not* to do when you want to talk dirty, and we will finally look at some bonus tips that you can use to help spice up your bedroom with minimal effort. You will drive your partner crazy for you, and all you have to do is learn how to talk to him or her.

Remember, keep an open mind as you read. You are not trying to learn to say things that make your partner feel bad; you are saying things that will bring your partner pleasure and enjoyment. Yes, you may be saying things that are offensive in the moment if you and the other person were in any other situation, but oftentimes, in the moment when you are bent over, or have the other person bent over, it can be incredibly erotic to be called a name. It can be erotic to tell someone to suck your cock in the right context, or it can be horribly offensive.

Dirty talk does not come easily for everyone, and some times, it can be more difficult to use than people would expect, but you can usually work through it and become an expert at turning your partner on with just your words. You can use just those simple words to bring the other person to their knees, maybe even literally, just by knowing all the right things to say.

Keep in mind that this book is, by no means, supposed to make you an expert at sex, nor is it a medical guide to try to up your performance. It is here as a reference with all sorts of suggestions that will help you spice up your sex life and drive your partner crazy. Will all of these suggestions work on each and every individual person? Probably not—but they are worth a try.

Chapter 1: Introducing Dirty Talk

Imagine this. You're in the mood, but your partner is sitting across from you on the couch, reading a book, and not seeming interested in the least. What do you do? You could say, "Hey, get over here, let's bang," but let's be real here—is that going to work? For some people, maybe. Some people are totally happy to jump to it and get some without having to work up to anything. There are some that are always DTF. But, that is not always the case by any means. Telling your partner to get over here and fuck you is probably not always going to work, and even if that does work for you right off the bat, there is a chance that just a quick session of wham, bam, thank you ma'am (or sir), is not going to do it.

If your partner is not really in to just being summoned for sex, then doing so will not help you. If your partner is okay with that, you may find that you want to bring your sex life to the next level. Thankfully, you can do both quite simply—all by mastering the art of dirty talk. If you can use dirty talk the right way, you can turn your partner on so much easier than you would probably realize. It is not some crazy, magical act that can only be done in the bedroom either—you can use it to build up that sexual tension to drive your partner wild. All you have to do is know how to use it tactfully.

What Is Dirty Talk?

Dirty talk itself is not inherently dirty in any way. It does not have to be aggressive, violent, disrespectful, or anything else—it is literally just speaking about sex. It is basically just being willing to talk about erotically. Like sex, it is just as personal to the individual receiving it. Not every person is approached in the same way, and you need to be able to tailor what you are saying to the person. It can be offensive to one person or highly erotic to another, and may even vary based on the context

Of course, however, you still have to learn how to do it in the first place. Just as sex requires exploration and learning how to perform and how to create the best time for both you and your partner, you will have to experiment with your partner and talk about what you both like and what you don't, but eventually, you will have it down to an art. You will create the right kind of talk that will drive both of you insane, and you will love it. It supercharges the tension in the air and can really help to elevate the experience.

Dirty talk is surprisingly easy to use—in general; it is as simple as saying what you want and what you like. This essentially allows you to describe what you like at any point in time so that you can drive your partner wild. Men love to watch what they are doing. Women love to hear what is liked. This means that if your partner is a woman, they are already likely to be highly susceptible to the talk in the first place—they will love to hear what you are enjoying.

We will be addressing dirty talk for men and women later on in this book, but ultimately, women are going to take more work to build up to the fullest potential pleasure that they could enjoy. This means that if you want to heat things up quickly, dirty talk is your best bet.

Is It Inherently Disrespectful?

Of course, you may have your own reservations. If the idea of calling your partner crude names and demanding that they do lewd things to you is not your idea of a good time, or if your partner is not receptive to that, you can still talk dirty. There are no rules that say that your words have to be disrespectful or even particularly derogatory. Even saying things like, "Wow, you feel so good," or, "I love it when you move like that," constitutes dirty talk—and that kind of feedback can drive someone insane if you can do it just right.

Of course, it may be that in the moment, you and your partner genuinely do enjoy being more forceful or enjoy being able to call each other names. We all have different interests, and if you and your partner decide that you are into it, that is fine, too. There is nothing wrong with calling your partner a slut if your partner is receptive to it in the moment, and it serves to turn your partner on, and you both consent to it, it is fine. Just as with any other sexual act, all that matters is that both parties are willing.

Bringing Up the Idea of Dirty Talk

When it comes to bringing up the idea of dirty talk, you may be lost. It can be difficult to figure out where to begin, or even if your partner is going to be receptive in the first place. Not everyone is, but you can usually begin to figure out how to understand your partner with some experience. Think about your first time in bed with your partner. Was it great? For most people, first sexual experiences with a new partner rarely are as good as those that happen long after the fiery passion of the honeymoon period is gone, and why is that? Because you learn what turns each other on!

You learn exactly where all of those little physical buttons to press on your partner ar. You learn what he or she likes and what is disliked. You learn what is going to help them get the best orgasm that they can and what is going to ultimately lead to them not finishing at all, unsatisfied and annoyed. It's only natural— you won't know how someone else's body works until you have had the time to experiment with them. It is only then when you learn how their body works, or if you have very explicit instructions on what they like, that you can actually do what they want when they want it the first time.

You need to go through the same learning process with the mind as well. Some keywords may be enough to drive your partner wild, or some words may just be an immediate turn off depending upon their past experiences, and you will need to figure that out with time. If you can go through the struggle of learning what they like, you will be able to really enjoy each other. You can do this by talking about it. Dirty talk really is nothing but asking each other what you like and what you do not. It is talking about what you want to do and what you do not want to do. You can start off incredibly lightly at first, slowly working up to something a bit more intense when you have gotten good responses.

Light dirty talk

To begin with, you want to start with some basic talk. Imagine this; for example—you are at work and really wishing that you could get your hands all over your partner. You could text a quick message saying, "I miss you," or even with a winky emoji added to it or something else suggestive. Or, you could ramp it up a bit. Instead of something not particularly explicit, you would instead send them a message stating, "I miss the feeling of your tits in my hand," or something else similar. NSFW? Sure. But there is nothing particularly demeaning or even shocking in that particular message. You are telling your partner what it is that you miss and what you want. This is one of the unspoken rules of dirty talk; you have to be willing to tell them what you want in the moment so that you can get it, and because you are telling your partner that you want them, you are turning them on too.

Pay attention to how they respond to these light messages of what you want. It is important that you know what it is that your partner will be receptive to. Usually, early dirty talk is much more innocent, so to speak—it is talking about what you like and is usually more affectionate. It involves messages such as:

- I love the way you feel
- I need your body right now
- I'm so turned on by you right now
- I love your hands right there
- You look so sexy right now
- I love what you are doing right this moment
- You feel so good

You usually won't see many protests to most of this dirty talk; in fact, if you tell your partner that he or she is driving you wild, they will probably respond well to you. They will feel that tension building within them, and you will probably have a better time.

Moderate dirty talk

After enough light, dirty talk, it is time to consider some more moderate talk. This is usually a bit more explicit. You may find that at this stage, your partner gets even more excited in the moment, or you may find that you have reached that boundary point, especially if your partner voices that he or she feels taken advantage of, dirty, annoyed, or unhappy with any of this talk. However, if your partner responds well and seems to be turned on, even more, you know that you are on the right track. These are phrases such as:

- I want to dominate you/I want you to dominate me
- You have the perfect pussy/cock
- I love how you ride me
- Fuck me louder
- I'm going to pound you tonight
- I want you to pound me harder with your big dick/cock
- I love sucking your cock/licking your pussy so much

As you can see, at this level, you are getting a bit more explicit. You are starting to use words that, in ordinary circumstances, would be deemed vulgar or inappropriate. They can be offensive to some people, so you will need to make sure that you know where your partner draws that line.

X-rated dirty talk

Here, you are looking at dirty talk that usually is not going to be brought into a relationship that is still new. You are using this kind of talk for a partner that you know is going to be comfortable with it, and usually, you want to slowly build up to this, if your partner is receptive. This is overtly sexual; it is the kind of talk that is going to only be reserved for talking behind closed doors, or possibly through texts in private, but these are not phrases that would, under any means, be appropriate in any context beyond sex with someone.

- Show me how wet my slutty little pussy is
- Fuck me harder
- I want to be your little fuck toy
- I want to ruin your pussy
- I want you to ruin my pussy
- I want you to fuck me harder
- I want to taste myself on you

Some people are into this, but others would balk at such talk at any point in their relationship. It is important to recognize that everyone has their own boundaries that you will need to respect. Dirty talk, even when based in this kind of language, should still be adhering to the boundaries of your partner. Sex is intimate, even amongst strangers or during one night stands. It is a deeply personal act to give your body to someone else, and no matter the context, no matter if you are into BDSM, talking dirty, or anything else, the important part to emphasize is always consent and boundaries. Of course, you only know what those boundaries are if you can talk to the other person to figure out what theirs are in the first place. Communication is key.

Tips for Introducing Dirty Talk

So, you want to add dirty talk into your relationship. It could be great fun for you and your partner, and there is a good chance that you will find something that works for both of you. It may feel intimidating, but the best thing that you can do is get started. Start small and work up to what it is that you want to do. Make sure that you ask your partner during times that are not sexually charged about their own preferences and if anything stood out to them during your last romp.

If you are getting ready and don't know where to start to introduce dirty talk, then pay attention to these tips that are being provided for you. They are great starting points to begin talking about what it is that you and your partner want out of your relationship, how far you are both willing to go, and how you can both get the most potential enjoyment out of it. Try it and start slow—you will probably find that your sex gets even hotter than it ever was.

Talk about what you want

When it comes right down to it, you should make sure that you always talk about what it is that you want. When you are sending messages to your partner, or even just talking to him or her when you are not able to actually get down to business, you can drop little hints to drive the other person crazy. Tell your partner what you want. "I want you right now." "I wish I could feel your hands on me." "I miss the way that your breasts/hips/ass feels." Those are all starting points—you are telling your partner what you ideally want at that point in time, and that will drive them wild.

During sex, tell your partner what you like

During the actual act, make sure that you give feedback to your partner. Tell them what you like. Tell them what is really working for you. Make sure that you tell them what it is that you want if what they are doing is not quite doing it for you. Dirty talk is there to bridge that gap in communication. It is there to get comfortable with the idea of communicating about your own sexual desires and preferences without feeling ashamed or bothered by it, while simultaneously setting the stage for it.

Talk about it before the moment

Make sure that you have some time before you even begin to use it, where you and your partner have a genuine discussion of what you want out of your sex that you are having and what you like to hear or what you dislike hearing. Maybe there are some words that simply drive you insane, and not in a good way—before you begin to add dirty talk to your relationship is the best time to go over that. Make sure that you are communicating effectively.

Learn to be assertive

You have to be assertive in sex. Make sure that you are able to tell your partner exactly what you want or what you do not want. If they ask you if they can cum on your face, but you say that you are not into that, fair enough. You need to be able to say no, or say, "Hey, what you're doing really isn't for me. Let's forget about that." It is okay for you to say no about something that you do not care to do; in fact, you should say no to avoid resentment, which will destroy your relationship far quicker than anything else.

Don't be afraid to ask for something

Similarly, make sure that if there is something that you really want, you need to be willing to communicate about it. Don't hesitate to ask if something that you want is in your mind; you can always ask. Worst case scenario, you are told no, but really, that's better than feeling like you're denying yourself because you are too shy to ask.

Get creative

Make sure that you are using adjectives to describe what you are feeling. Think about the way that you want to describe your partner and see how he or she responds. Are they turned on when you tell them that they are beautiful/handsome, or do they respond better being called dirty or naughty? Everyone has different preferences, and the sooner that you can figure out what your partner's preferences are, the sooner you can begin to use them to entice them.

Don't forget your verbs

Yes, what you are doing is fucking—but use some other words in there too. Make a call to action. Talk about what you want and use verbs that will paint the picture of what you want. After all, "I want to make sweet love to you," has a totally different connotation than, "I want to fuck you so hard that you won't be able to walk tomorrow." Think about what it is that you prefer to talk about and also what appeals to your partner.

Compliment your partner in the moment

In the moment, make sure that you offer your partner compliments. What are they doing that drives you crazy? What makes you hotter? Do you like how they are moving or what they are doing? Compliment it? "God, your hair looks so damn sexy when you're on me," or "Wow, your touch feels so good." When you do this, you let your partner know that you are, in fact, enjoying every moment of what you are doing with them, and that will turn most people on more than anything else.

Narrate what you will do

Another great starting point is to narrate what you are about to do. Make sure that you, in the moment, let your partner know what you are about to do or what you are doing. "I'm gonna fuck you so hard right now," just before you start, or "Fuck, I'm gonna cum" or something along those lines. When you narrate like that, you put your partner in your mind as well. You are showing them the idea that you are enjoying what is happening. You are showing your partner how much you are having fun, and that matters in the moment.

Check in after sex

Dirty talk doesn't end when the fun does—you also need to talk to your partner after the fact.

This is a sort of aftercare; it helps to show that your partner matters to you, and that will help to enhance what happened. You can talk to your partner about the actions that you enjoyed or tell your partner what they did so well, and you let them know that you continue to think about them and the fun that you had after the fact.

Take some of your dirty talk outside of the bedroom

When you are standing with your partner while doing something together, don't forget to add in your double entendres here and there to remind them that you are thinking about what you are doing. Even innocent comments can do the job for you. Imagine that your partner wears a deodorant that smells very distinct; perhaps it is a floral one. When you are at the grocery store talking about the candles and trying to choose one out, you can point out one that smells similarly and make a comment about it that lets your partner know that you are thinking about them, their scent, and the passionate fun you had in bed.

Experiment often

If you and your partner are still trying to figure out what it is that you want or like, you can, and should, experiment often. Bring new talk to the bedroom and mention it when you talk. Bring your desires to life all around you. Talk about what you want to do when you get the chance to do so.

Find inspiration

Sometimes, you will see some things that are highly erotic on television, or you'll read a book that has a particularly provocative line in it. Keep in mind that ultimately, television, books, and porn are just fiction—but the words used can still be deeply powerful and can be highly erotic as well. If you are having a hard time coming up with the right words to use, you can make sure that you do talk the right way to the person that you are around.

Get used to talking about sex in all sorts of contexts

A great way to help yourself figure out what you can do to eliminate some of the taboo is to start talking to your friends as well. No, you probably won't be telling your friends that you want to take them, bend them over, and fuck them, but if you can get used to saying so many of those words on your own even in normal conversations, you will be more able to talk to your partner as well. You need to be able to say words that you will need to use in the moment with them.

Expand your vocabulary

Another great starting point is to figure out the words that you are comfortable using. Make sure that you have a list of those that you won't mind making use of regularly. It could be that you are fine calling a penis a dick, but if calling a vagina a pussy or a cunt is a problem, figure out what you do want to call it. There is no right or wrong answer here for you; you can choose the one that is just right for you.

Keep it simple

You don't have to start off talking like you are in the middle of a porno—make sure that you are using words that you are comfortable with, and you can even keep it short. As you walk past your partner, whisper, "I can't wait to have you," for example—that could be enough to drive him or her insane. You don't have to do anything uniquely spectacular or creative or spout off a long ode to your partner's genitalia to constitute dirty talk. Even the occasional comment could be enough for you and your partner to get off better than before.

Channel your senses

When you are thinking of saying something, make sure that you use something that plays on the senses. Sex is intensely sensual, and you want to bring the senses into things as much as you can. "I can't wait for tonight." "I need to taste you." I want to feel you." I love how you smell." Try to hit all of the senses when you are getting started.

Start slowly

You don't have to just rush into things to have good dirty talk. In fact, some of the best, especially early on, involves slowly adding it in. Bring it up, little by little, and tell your partner what you like and what you want. You'll be surprised at the end results.

Be playful

There should not be anything innately hurtful; it should all be in good fun. If you want to enjoy your relationship with your partner, you want to make sure that ultimately, you are using your dirty talk to spice things up and make things more enjoyable. There is no reason to make yourself or your partner feel bad.

Give instructions

It can help to stop and tell your partner exactly what you want in the moment. Instead of asking for it, tell them what you want. This is a great way to really get them in the mood. A lot of people like it when their partner takes charge and tells them what to do; they are happy to comply. If you are interested in something, you should tell your partner what you want.

Try roleplaying

Some people find that the dirty talk, in general, is simpler if they are getting into the mood through roleplay instead. You can ask if you and your partner can try a small roleplay scenario and see if that gets the words flowing.

Try via text or messages if you feel too self-conscious

Now, it may just be that you cannot look at your partner with a straight face and say, "I want you to fuck me. Hard. Right now." Fine, fair enough. It can take time to work up to something like that. But, what you can do is begin to send some suggestive messages. Leave a note in your partner's lunch or in their car to find. Send a text when you know they won't get in trouble.

If something doesn't work, talk about it later

If you find that you have said something to your partner that immediately kills the mood, ask about it later. It might not be something that you can talk about in the moment, but you can usually check in with your partner after the fact. It is important that when you are in a sexual relationship, you are able to check in after the fact, and if you get the idea that you have made a mistake, make sure you ask about it later.

Figure out their sexual triggers

Figure out what it is that your partner really wants. Figure out the language that gets them rearing to go and make sure that you use them regularly. Most people have certain terms that they use, and you should figure those out. What do they say to you when they talk about sex? Do they call it sex? Fucking? Love-making? You want to adopt their language surrounding everything.

Let them know how turned on you are

You should always let your partner know when you want to use dirty talk, when, and how turned on you are. You can let them know what you are feeling, and that brings awareness to it. You are making them feel better because they feel like they can be more confident with you; they feel like fucking you is that much more fun because you are giving them that little ego boost.

One-word dirty talk

Sometimes, all you need is one word. You can say, "Yes," or "Harder," or "Deeper." When you add just one word, your partner knows that they are doing a good job; you weren't able to say a complete sentence, and they know that you are enjoying it. Master this, and don't be afraid to whisper it to them as you go.

Ask them what they want

Sometimes, you can make things sexier in the moment when you ask your partner what they want you to do. "How do you want me to finish you off?" or "How do you want to cum tonight?" are great in the heat of the moment, and you are letting your partner know that you will take care of him/her.

Use it when your partner least expects it

One thing that you can do to consistently get others off is to let them know that you want to do something when they least expect it. Send a quick message that says, "I want your pants off when I get home," or something similar, and you tell your partner that you are thinking about them.

Use it often

Make sure that you are willing to talk regularly about what you want. This is a great way to build up that tension all day long and get your partner's engines revving and juices flowing. If you want a good fuck, make them want it.

Do some research

You can learn all about what to say and find new lines pretty easily. You can find online erotica and read over that to get some inspiration. You can get all sorts of new phrases that can be used there, and your partner may even go crazy for them.

Chapter 2: Dirty Talk as Foreplay

Men may be able to go from 0 to ready to go to the bone zone in an instant, but that doesn't mean that they *should*. Why rush to the end? Foreplay is defined as sexual activity of any kind before the actual act of sexual intercourse. Some people prefer foreplay—a lot, and for a good reason. Foreplay is like the appetizer before the main course. It is there to help your partner, and you both enjoy sexual acts more. Your body is not primed to always enjoy sex—there are certain criteria that have to happen. Think about it—have you ever had sex when you were not ready, if you are a woman, or if you are a man, have you ever tried to slide in before your partner was ready? Or before you were yourself? You can't—or if you can, it is not pleasant.

Arousal happens during the foreplay stage. Your body, and your partner's, prepare for sex, and as a result, you and your partner both end up enjoying it that much more as a result. Men get harder. They find that they have more sensation during the act. Women get wetter, making everything that much more enjoyable as well. Blood flows down to the genitalia during arousal, and as a result, everything feels better.

Foreplay is so important—you need it if you want to have good sex. Can you have good sex if you and your partner both happen to be insanely horny at the same time without needing that setup? Sure—but that is the exception more than the rule. If you want good, passionate sex, do not forget the foreplay.

Foreplay doesn't have to be physical, and it doesn't have to happen immediately before you actually have sex. In fact, you can enjoy it all day long, tantalizingly teasing your partner so that you know their blood is rushing, and they are ready for that end of the night finale. It will probably become even more sensual when you have had all day long to drive your partner absolutely crazy with your talk and with your actions. All you have to do is know how to turn your partner on.

Turning Your Partner on With Dirty Talk

During arousal, all sorts of different things happen in the body. Your body literally prepares for the act of sex when it is aroused—it prepares the proper responses that your body will need. Your heart rate increases, along with blood pressure and pulse—this makes sense if blood is being redirected to the genitalia to help with sensation. Likewise, blood vessels will dilate in the genitals so that they can become engorged with blood. The penis swells up as a result, and on women, both the clitoris and labia do as well. For women, the breasts will also swell up, and nipples become erect, and the vagina becomes lubricated naturally.

All of this happens so that the body is ready to have and enjoy sex. It is only when you are actually aroused that sex is actually enjoyable in the first place, and if you are not, you may come to enjoy it in the moment, or you simply dislike it the entire time. Either can happen as a result of what is going on. But really, do you want to enjoy your time? Start with the foreplay. It will put you in the right mood as well. You will be able to build the emotional intimacy that all good sexual relationships need, and you will also be able to lower inhibitions during the foreplay. It is intoxicating and heady, and the more that you play around with each other, physically or verbally, the better your sex will go. Foreplay helps to release the necessary hormones that will lower cortisol—the stress hormone—in preparation for the bonding and affection felt during the act of sex.

Better Sex With Dirty Talk

Foreplay is important—there is no doubt about that. But, if you want to have better sex with dirty talk, you can make it happen. Dirty talk makes sex better just because of the way that it works. We want to be lusted after. We want to feel like we are wanted. We want to believe that our bodies drive our partners insane and that our partners want to get back with us as soon as possible. It's not just about going through the motions; it is about the fiery passion and pleasure. It is about taking someone else's body and making it your own. It is about enjoying yourself more intimately than possible in other ways. Sex is fun, but there is so much more to it than that. It is inherently programmed into us, and it is there to make us bond with our partners. It creates those feelings of euphoria and affection that we associate with our partners. Foreplay and dirty talk will both elevate sex from "meh" to being hot and better than ever before.

Dirty talk makes sex better—we know that for sure. We also know why it does that as well. Let's talk about the ways that dirty talk can create a better sex experience for both you and your partner before we continue on with looking at how to make it happen.

You can tell your partner what you like and dislike

Good sex, the kind that blows your mind, is all about communication—so why not make that communication fun and pleasant? Why not make that communication something enjoyable? Why not make sure that the communication does the work for you as well? You could tell your partner one day that the sex that you have is great when they do that one thing, or you could tell your partner in the moment, "Oh, god, I love it when you do that!"

as it is happening. Telling your partner in the moment is going to leave them on fire; it will automatically stoke their inner fire. They know that what they are doing right in that moment is working for you, and that is enough for them.

You are able to connect better

Sex is also about connection. Even with one-night stands, you are still making a connection between yourself and the other person to some degree; you are able to tell your partner what it is that you want or need out of the encounter. Connection matters and dirty talk can help foster it.

You can reignite a lost flame

If you are living with your long-term partner, you may find that your infatuation, that highly passionate, desire-laden feeling is replaced with something that feels less. All too many people will mistake what happens to their feelings with them losing their love for the other person. However, it is normal for infatuation to disappear. However, you can spark that flame of passion again in the bedroom. Dirty talk can help you find those feelings of lust that you thought faded away with the infatuation. With a bit of dirty talk, you can add some variety to the relationship so that you are able to maintain that spark and enjoyment with each other.

It is versatile

Even if you and your partner are not together right at that moment for any reason, whether they have to work or they have traveled or anything else, you can send them pictures that remind them that they are the one for you and that you want them more than they probably realize. You are able to figure out what it will take for you and your partner to keep that spark alight, and you will be able to help create that allure; your partner will be caught up with you and probably spend all day long, thinking about getting back to your bed.

You'll boost your confidence

The act of talking to your partner and seeing the effect that it has on him, or her is a great boost in confidence. If you want to make sure that you are confident, you want to make sure that you can confirm that your partner is attracted to you, and a wonderful way to make that happen is through the way that you talk dirty to him or her. It will make you feel so much better about yourself when you realize that the simple act of talking to your partner is enough to drive him or her wild.

You'll also feel more attractive as a result as well. You'll feel like, in saying those words, you can take control, and you can get exactly what you want when you want it, and that is highly compelling and powerful.

It creates variety

If you can talk dirty to each other, you are able to make sure that your sex life never gets boring. You and your partner are able to figure out everything that you will need to do to maintain your passion for each other. You will be able to try new things and really and truly enjoy them as much as possible to really make sure that your spark never fades.

You can use dirty talk as a segue into talking about new positions, bringing toys into the relationship, and even starting to experiment with new objects. It can help you transition to speaking about, and therefore trying, any of those kinks that you may have had but been afraid to talk about. You will be able to tell your partner about those things that you have kept hidden, not knowing how to bring it up.

It makes you feel better about what you are doing in the moment

When you and your partner can talk to each other about intimate acts like sex, you know that you can talk about just about anything, including aspects of your life. You can alleviate the pressure that comes along with sex—you do not feel like your performance is under complete scrutiny in the moment because you and your partner are both talking about your actions with each other. Your partner is saying what he or she likes and that will give you that boost that you needed to know to help yourself figure out that you do not actually have to worry about the pressure aspect of what is happening. You aren't worrying about if you are doing things right because you can see that ultimately, your partner must be into it if they are dirty talking back.

It makes sex feel better

Sex is not designed to be quiet. Think about it— we groan and moan and grunt sometimes. It is not something that is meant to be prim and proper—it is us giving into our carnal, most feral desires that we have, and that means letting go of needing to be quiet. When you tell your partner how good things feel, you help make it feel even better. You make it real by acknowledging it, elevating it to the next level. This also helps you to create that higher sense of fulfillment that you are looking for as well.

Ultimately, sex is better with dirty talk. We love it—it lets us communicate what matters the most, and it helps us to feel more in tune with our desires. That is highly important to consider, and the sooner that we recognize that, the better. Give it a shot. Let your shame or embarrassment go and talk dirty to your partner. You'll be surprised by how different things can be with it.

Creating Sexual Tension with Dirty Talk

Sexual tension is highly powerful. We see it used in media all of the time because of the effect that it has—it's *hot*. It's so fun to see the ways that people respond to each other when they clearly want to have sex, but are afraid to or they can't, or there is some sort of boundary that cannot be crossed. It typically involves delaying or denying sex. The sex could cause problems, such as at work, or because there is a reason that it would otherwise have social impacts that are wanted to be avoided.

In relationships, however, sexual tension occurs when two people want to have sex and are flirting but can't actually perform for some reason. Maybe you and your partner are both at a big family event, and there is no way to comfortably give in without being caught. Maybe you and your partner are staying in someone else's home, or your children are around, or you're apart for work. No matter the reason, however, you can encourage sexual tension.

While sexual tension between two people that are not sexual partners may be awkward and uncomfortable, in a relationship or with partners, it can help you maintain that hot sex life that keeps both of you going crazy for each other. If you want to be able to build your own sexual tension, you need to know how to make it happen, and usually, it should be happening all day long.

The longer you can stoke that tension, the better it will feel when you release it. After all, what is orgasm other than a sudden release of built-up tension? You can build that tension up higher and higher all day long if you know how to get started. Dirty talk is one of the easiest ways to begin building that tension so that when you get home or when you and your partner are with each other again, you will not be able to keep your hands off of each other.

If you want to create tension, all you have to do is follow some simple ideas, and usually, dirty talk is the easiest way to do so, especially if you and your partner are apart from each other. Your ability to create that tension is going to make your partner completely and utterly addicted to you, and you will be able to guarantee that they will not be able to keep their hands away. If you want that, if you want to know that your partner will be vying to get that release from you any way possible, keep in mind the idea of creating sexual tension.

Start in the morning and keep it going all day

One thing that you need to do if you want to keep that tension going all day long is to start first thing in the morning. We all usually rush through the morning; it is hard to really have time for each other when we have places to go and maybe even kids to shuttle around. But, the morning is the perfect time to start that fire. You can create that spark, leaving the orgasm for later, allowing you to continually stoke the spark until your partner can't stand it any longer.

As you're getting ready to part in the morning, whisper a few dirty phrases to your partner, even if you don't have the time to sit down and make it happen. If you can remind each other of what you are doing and what you think, whispering those phrases of sweet passion to each other, you can get that flame stoked, and in no time, they will be begging for you as soon as you reunite.

Send texts throughout the day

When you have a thought about your partner during the day, let them know. Remind them that you are thinking about them. Tell yourself that you can't wait to get them in bed with you. If you miss them, tell them what you want to do. They will love the little boost in their ego first thing in the morning. You could even slip in a quick picture if you wanted to; they will probably love it.

Get creative with your timing

If you want that tension to build, make sure that you are getting creative. If you are in the theater, you can whisper a comment that will make them blush, and you will probably instantly turn them on. A well-placed hand on a thigh with the right look and the right phrase will build up that tension and make it impossible to forget it. You will be able to make sure that ultimately, they can't stop thinking about you, and that is exactly what you need. If you want to make sure that your partner craves you and will do whatever it is that you want them to, this is one way to drive them insane.

Whisper in their ear or in the crook of their neck

You want to make sure that your partner will be as turned on as possible, and that means that you will want to use all of their senses. Hovering right by their ear and whispering to them when you can to deliver that moment of what you want them to hear is the greatest way to really deliver that double whammy of physical closeness, whispering in an erogenous zone, and then also saying something that you know is going to turn them on.

Tips for Dirty Talk

Now, if you want to start delivering the best possible dirty talk that you can to your partner, it is time to get down to business through all sorts of different tips and tricks that you can use. If you really want to drive your partner insane, you need to be able to use the right words to make sure that they really want you. We are going to go over another 30 tips right now that will help you to bring your dirty talk to the next level during your relationship. You will be able to take your foreplay from average levels to those that are burning with desire that will make that moment of release that much sweeter when you are finally able to satisfy that desire that you have for your partner.

Make it authentic

When you are using dirty talk, make sure that what you say is authentic. If you are really thinking about fucking your partner's brains out, then say that—or if you are thinking about that quiet sensual night that you had the other night, tell them that, too. You should not be afraid of what it is that you are going to say to your partner. Make sure that you are paying attention to the way that your authenticity is being received as well.

Make sure it is mirroring your partner

Watch your partner—pay attention to if they seem to want to engage. If they engage after you have reached out and left a sexual line to grab, then go ahead and continue. If they seem not to be into it for some reason, pushing probably is going to do more harm than good. Make sure that if your partner is the first one to reach out, you reciprocate as well.

Ask simple questions

If you are asking questions at all to be erotic, make sure that the questions that you ask are those that are simple to answer—they should be yes or no questions. Your partner is not looking to be quizzed—rather, he or she probably wants to enjoy the moment and asking too many times how they like something is probably going to kill the moment. Instead of texting your partner saying, "What do you want me to do tonight?" which would put them on the spot and may be difficult for them to answer, you can ask, "Do you want me to fuck you hard tonight?"

Build up to it gradually

If you are building up your foreplay, even for the day, don't just jump straight for the X-rated script that you are thinking about; instead, build up over time, all day long. Start out with a quick whisper of, "I can't wait to get my hands on you tonight," for example, as you are passing by each other to go to work or wherever you go in the morning. Even if it might feel like a good idea to share your passion by saying,

"Goodbye, you dirty slut, I'll punish you accordingly when you get home," as you're walking out the door, if your partner isn't feeling it in the moment, you're probably going to do more harm than good. Start out innocently and build up all day long. It's not a race to incinerate everything; slow and steady is always best when you have a whole day of tantalizing messages to share.

Skip the eye contact at first if it is making you uncomfortable

Eye contact can be intense for people, especially if it is not something that they are usually comfortable with. However, you do not have to maintain eye contact for dirty talk. In fact, you can even have dirty talk occurring entirely over digital means without having to see each other in person at all if you wanted to. You can talk to them separately if you wanted to. You don't even have to look at the other person if it is making you nervous. If you find that you lack the confidence that you will need to get to the sexy point that you want to make, find a way to skip out on the eye contact. You can build up to that over time.

Make a promise for later, and follow through with it

If you tell your partner that you plan on bending them over and thrusting with reckless abandon that night during your constant foreplay for the day, you will want to follow through with it. Make that anticipation and reward it later on. Make sure that you always follow through with what you say that you are going to do so that you can make sure that ultimately when you tell your partner something, they know that you will follow through with it.

Inside jokes

Now, jokes may seem like the least sexy thing ever, but think of it this way—when you have inside jokes that are about your sex life, just mentioning the inside joke, or referencing it, can be enough to get your partner going with just a glance and a passing comment and no one else around you will be any wiser to what has just occurred. This is a fantastic way to approach the situation if you are trying to figure out how best to interact in ways that are not overt.

Say something with a double entendre

Imagine that you are eating a popsicle, sensuously sucking on it while making fuck-me eyes at your partner, smirking and saying that, "It tastes so good," or "Mmm..." as you do it. This is going to get your partner desperate for you without ever saying anything that is not really appropriate. The tone is what matters here, and the double entendre is probably enough to help your partner really feel like you want them. This is perfect. You could even lean over and mention something about wishing that you had them in your mouth instead.

Say something subtly possessive

Now, too much possessiveness and jealousy is obviously a problem in a relationship, but if you can play it off the right way and whisper it to your partner as you do, smirking, or flirting with them, you can drive them crazy. We innately like the idea of our partners claiming us as their own, especially when we know that it is not something that is meant from a bad place. It can be kind of sexy to hear our partners stake their claims over us, after all, especially if it is something like, "I want to make you mine."

It's all about the tone

Keep in mind that the tone of what you say is everything. If you want to drive your partner crazy, you have to use the right tone of voice, or you are going to find that he or she is probably going to lose interest. Think about it: would it be sexy for someone to tell you in a flat voice, "I love your cock/pussy."? No enthusiasm. No actual sense of enjoyment in there. Just a flat, robotic, "I love it." Would you believe it? Probably not. Would it stoke that fire within you? Probably not.

You need to master the sexy tone to master the art of foreplay, and that means making sure that your tone is something that you know they will find attractive. Go for something lower, throatier, and softer. Learn the voice. It's your sexy voice. Use it.

Read erotica to each other

If you and your partner are still struggling with being able to talk to each other honestly and from that point of sexual tension, then stop, take some time, and read some erotica that you can read back and forth to each other. This lets you get a feel for the writing and the phrasing. You start to adjust to saying the words in your mouth, and as a result, you get closer to stepping into the zone of being able to use your own dirty talk.

Be bold and take a chance

You never know how your partner will take what you are saying. Try taking some chances and saying some things that ordinarily, you wouldn't say, but that you decided to try out. Be bold. Say things that you think are hot, but that you wouldn't dare to say to your partner normally and see how he or she responds to it. You may be pleasantly surprised.

Make a game out of it

It could be fun to make a game out of trying to make each other blush. The point is to ramp up your sex talk until one of you or the other is blushing. Then, the other person is the winner in the situation. It can be fun trying to think of the sexiest, most blush-worthy comment that you can come up with in hopes of seeing what happens next.

Don't be ashamed as you talk

Don't worry about what you are saying; you are talking with someone that you have had sex with—you don't get much more vulnerable than having someone else's body part in you, or in putting your body part inside of someone else. Allow yourself to really come to terms with the sexual content that you are saying and don't mind it. You're saying things that are typically "inappropriate," but you have a very specific purpose for doing so—you are trying to turn on your partner. Let's face it—the act of sex itself, to someone who is not turned on, may seem a bit strange. It is messy and sweaty, and isn't it a little bit strange how we put our private bits together, and they somehow fit? Sex is strange. Nature is strange. The worlds that you use to try to turn someone on are probably going to seem strange too—but they serve a purpose. Let go of the shame and just do it.

Ask some dirty questions

Sometimes, it can help to ask questions that are dirty. "What do you think I'm wearing? How would you feel if I answered the door and was naked? What should I wear today for you?" Ask questions that start to hint on suggestive but are not all the way there yet. It starts to set the field for what you want to do—which is turn on your partner, and the sooner that you can do that, the sooner that you can get into bed.

Share your fantasies

If you have been dreaming or fantasizing about your partner, now is the time to share it. Talk to your partner about the dreams that you have been having or about what you want to do with your partner more than anything and don't hold back about it—the fantasies should be erotic, and you may find that your partner will even agree to do what you want to do without complaint. You may even find that you both share the same common fantasy!

Ask if your partner wants to take charge

If you want your partner to love fucking you, then you want to ask them if they want to be in control. Even if you are usually the one that takes the lead, ask them what they want. Figure out if they do want to be in the lead, and if they do, let it happen. You may find that you are pleasantly surprised by what happens next.

Tell your partner what you want them to do

If your partner is at home and you are at work, you can send them some sexy texts telling them what you want them to do right at that moment. Make it erotic, but make sure that they don't quite finish up the job without you. Let them know that you want to save the best part for you at home and that you're thinking about them doing it. This builds up that tension for you, and for them, you are both going to be dying to get into each other's arms.

Ask them to play dirty truth or dare

Again, if you want to create foreplay with dirty talk, games can be a great tool to use. You can set up, so you and your partner both play together and see where things take you. If all of the topics are erotic, you will both probably find that pretty soon, you're both desperate for the other's touch, and that means that your job was very well done.

Message them when you're masturbating

If you're going solo for a session and are apart, consider sending some sexy messages letting them know that you're thinking about them— *really* thinking about them. They will probably go crazy for it, and you can find yourself loving every single moment of it. You will be able to tease them with messages such as, "Oh, it's too bad you're not here, I could use some help ;)" or something similar to that to let them know that even when you're on your own, and even with the entirety of the internet's near-infinite and ever-expanding collection of porn, you chose to think about your partner.

Sexy riddles

You can use sexual riddles that are fun, but still erotic and send them or whisper them to your partner all day long, really building up that foreplay before your grand finale. Riddles can be something silly like, "What's hot and [skin color] and all wrapped up, waiting for you?" or something more erotic as well. Be creative. Be silly about it, but most of all, be erotic and sensual.

Tell them what turns you on

Make sure that you let your partner know exactly what it is that you want to do. Tell them what turns you on more than anything else, and they will probably use that to their advantage later on. Even better, if you are sharing turn ons, just thinking about them will probably get some juices or blood flowing, if you catch my drift.

Tell them what they do to you

If your partner is driving you crazy, let them know. Tell them just how passionate you are for them and just how much knowing that you can't be inside of them, or have them inside of you, right that moment is driving you mad. If you can do this, telling them just how passionate you are, you can boost their egos while also setting up that sexual tension for later on as well.

Tell them what you intend to do when you see each other next/the next time you are in bed

Let them know exactly what you're going to do next—tell them, for example, that you're going to tease them all day long, or that you're going to suck them or lick them or fuck them, or anything else that you're interested in doing. It will get them going crazy for you as well, and you will be able to see just how strong of an effect that you have on your partner when you do it. This is highly erotic and something that many people love to hear as well.

Create a template

If you struggle with dirty talk, it can help to have a sort of template, where you simply follow the lead and fill in the blanks to make it work for you. You could, for example, use some talk about what you love when they do something. Try this format: I love [action] when you [describe the action]. This can help you to begin to get that process down so that you can properly voice your approval or what really matters the most to you when you're getting down to business.

Create IOUs

You can create little sexual IOUs for each other as well. You can whisper to your partner what you want them to do to you that night, as well as whisper to them your promises for what you will do for them when you are able to get down and dirty that evening. The idea here is to create that anticipation for the night—it should be enticing and should drive you both wild. Hearing what you are going to do to each other is a great way for that tension that you need during foreplay to really be built up.

Ask them what they do when they are masturbating

You can also ask your partner what they think about when they are flying solo as well. You can use this information, hearing about what they do with each other so that you can begin to use that when you do have sex. This is a great way to open up conversations and connections about what you both like as well. It is a wonderful influence if you need to make sure that you are both able to talk to each other openly, and even better, it can turn you both on—you get to fantasize about your partner touching him/herself, and your partner gets the added benefit of thinking about you doing what they do.

Let them know about your favorite body part they have

Think about your partner and what attracts you the most to them physically—then compliment them for that body part. Let them know that their stomach or their abs or their breasts drive you insane and tell them all about how much you think about those body parts and what they mean to you. When you do this regularly, you are not only boosting confidence for them; you are also letting them know that you care about them and that you are paying attention to what they look like and how you see them. This is crucial; if you want to have mind-blowing sex, they have to feel confident enough to believe that you are attracted to them.

Talk about your own anticipation

Tell them what you can hardly wait for. Let them know that you are anticipating them. The idea that they are being lusted over is going to be highly erotic for them, and they will likely respond incredibly positively to it, meaning that you'll be able to have all the fun in the world when you can get together. Comments like, "I can't wait to feel you," or "I'm picturing us together naked right now, and I can't wait until we're alone so we can be," are great at stoking those flames and igniting that passion you want.

Chapter 3: Dirty Talk for Men

So. You want to get down with a man, do you? Do you want to make him hard with just a few whispers or a few words typed into your phone? You can make that happen—all you have to do is know what to say, and you'll get his blood pumping in no time at all. As you read through this chapter, you are going to learn all about what it is that will turn on a man with next to no effort at all—all you have to do is be smart about the way that you choose to communicate with him.

Dirty talk can be especially difficult to muster for many women who may feel awkward about what they will be saying. If you're a woman, or even a shy man, hoping to get it on with the man of your dreams, you need to learn one thing: Confidence is sexy. Take control. Take command of the conversation. Make sure that when you talk to him, you are brave about it and that you are willing to go for it. Many men are sex-driven—it is just part of their hardwiring. They are born to fuck, and if they can't, they feel defeated. They may feel emasculated if it is not clear from what you are doing or how you sound that you are enjoying yourself. They want to know what you think of them, especially during sex itself, and they want to hear what you want them to do to you as well.

Whether it is a well-placed moan, a few whispered words of affirmation that he is, in fact, getting you off, or even screaming his name with abandon, head thrown back in sheer ecstasy as you ride him, you have options and dirty talk for men is absolutely not a one size fits all sort of thing. However, one thing is consistent. No matter what, men want to feel validated in knowing that you are satisfied with their sex, either in the moment, leading up to the moment, or even after the fact. All you have to do is figure out how to tell him that.

What Men Want to Hear

Men, when in bed, are simple creatures. They want to know that you are enjoying them, and they want to feel like they are getting you off. If you can give them that, you are already going to escalate the sex to fantastic levels that your partner will most likely thrive on. Think about it—how validating and how much of a turn on is it for you if you are told that your sex is the best, or if you can see that the other person is loving every moment with you?

When you are talking to your partner, then your dirty talk simply has to inform him of one thing: That you want him to fuck you because you think that sex with him is fantastic. If your dirty talk conveys that, you are probably on the right track just like that. How can you do that, then? Simple—you can tell him what you want to do, or you can make use of moans when making out or riding him. You can tell him that he is fucking you so good or that you love it. There are so many options there—you just have to let him know that you are there, present and in the moment and that you would rather be there than anywhere else.

Turning Men On

When it comes to turning your man on, you have no shortage of ways. You could simply take off your own clothes, and he will probably be hard just thinking about the time that he can have with you. You can kiss him or touch him or tell him to fuck you there, or you could do it the long way, building up that sexual tension and making it so that he can't think about anything else. Turning men on is more than just touching some cock and balls or shaking an ass. There are ways to do so without ever laying a finger on him, in fact, and some of those can be even sexier than what you may do to him in bed.

Remember that ultimately, every man is going to be different. Every man is going to have his own preferences that you will need to consider, but if you are able to consider them effectively, you can also usually make it happen in very similar ways through seduction. If you want to turn your man on, consider these options to get that blood pumping and get him ready to go.

Smile seductively

The seductive smile is a great way to get him going, especially if you have just said something that could fall into a double entendre zone. Giving him a quick, sexy smile, especially if you let your eyes undress him within his attention, can drive him wild. You can do this across a room from each other, or you can do it in the middle of a conversation. Make sure that you have an intense gaze as you look at him and try to entice him over.

Be confident

Confidence is sexy, whether you are a man or a woman. If you can speak with confidence, act with confidence, smile with confidence, and more, you will find that he absolutely loves the way that you engage with him. Make sure that, no matter what it is that you are saying to him, you do it with confidence. Even if you tell him something that sounds borderline ridiculous when you first say it, if you can pull it off, you will find that he will go crazy for you in an instant. All you have to do is have that confident attitude.

Compliment him

Men *love* to be complimented. It gives him that ego boost that will help to turn him on even more, and it also shows that you are paying attention to him, meaning that you are getting him ready with two different tactics at once. If you want to make sure that you can get him happy, hot, and in bed, you want to give him the best compliments that you can think of. Tell him how smart he is when he helps you. Let him know that you think he's sexy when he's doing something. When you're in bed together, tell him how you are enjoying it. All of this will help you to turn him on with ease, and the sooner that you turn him on, the sooner that you will find that he will want to stick by you.

Dress sexy

Of course, men also love their eye candy. If you want him to think that you look great, then you have to act the part as well. Make sure that you wear something that you know that he would love. If he is into tight, black dresses, try wearing one. If he is into something else, try wearing that for him. He will greatly appreciate the help and will probably not hesitate to look you over.

Show some skin

Similarly, spending some time showing skin can help a lot as well. Wear shorts, short skirts, or short dresses, and make sure that they are low-cut. In particular, men tend to go crazy for the breasts, thighs, ass, neck, and back. Those are some of the most common parts that can turn a man on almost immediately, especially if he already likes you. You just have to play your part and let him enjoy the moment.

Hold eye contact

Eye contact is sexy. It tells the other person that at that moment, they are the only person on your mind, and that is enough to turn them on, man or woman. When you are able to connect with someone else through maintained eye contact and making sure that he sees that you are interested, you will turn him on.

Whisper what you want with him

When it comes to getting him hard for you, you can tell him exactly what it is that you want. Whisper in his ear that you want to ride him, or that you want his cock in your mouth. If you can tell him what you want to do with him, you will be filling him up with all sorts of anticipation and sexual tension, and he will not be able to get enough of you. You will drive him wild, all through dirty talk.

Dirty Talk Foreplay with Men

Foreplay is great for men and women—it can be incredibly fulfilling to have someone all over your body or even just in your mind. Foreplay, however, does not have to be only physical. You can tease with your voice, with your words, and even over text if you want to. You just have to know what you are doing and let it happen.

If you want to engage in foreplay with your partner, start with your words. Make sure that you tell your partner what you want to do. Don't overthink things—just say what comes to mind. What do you want him to do to you? What do you want to do to him? What are you thinking about right that moment as you are watching and wanting him? Think about those things and then verbalize them. The foreplay follows. As you tell him what it is that you want, you are usually able to ensure that your partner gets turned on quicker and that they are anticipating the sex more so that it is also more enjoyable as a direct result.

You can also talk to him about your secret fantasies—tell him what you're really thinking about and what you really want to try doing, even if you are afraid that he might laugh. Remember, confidence is sexy, and if you want to be confident, the best way to do so is to know what you are saying and how to drive him wild. The more that you drag foreplay out, the more eager he will be to finally get his hands on you for the big event, and you will notice a world of difference.

Dirty Talk During Sex with Men

During sex, dirty talk is easy. Tell him what you like. Tell him what you want him to do. Be as vulgar as you want. There are, of course, some considerations to make. Does he like being called "daddy," or would he prefer that you use his name? Tell him when you are getting close to finishing up and tell him when you are really enjoying yourself. The more that you can communicate how you are doing in the moment, the more turned on he will be as a direct result. If you want him to fuck you, tell him that. If you want him to go quicker or slower, tell him that as well.

Some men may prefer to be the ones in charge, but most of the time, they can respect being told what to do and how to do it. It can be sexy to be commanded about in bed, and men love that. If you really want to turn him on, and you want to do it well, you will be explicitly clear about what you want.

One thing to consider, however, is that you shouldn't try to censor yourself. Keep it vulgar. Keep it derogatory. Tell him that you want his cock inside of you, not that you want his genitals within your own. You want to make sure that it doesn't get awkward and going from sexy small talk to suddenly using anatomically correct terms can be a bit of a mood killer.

Steps to Dirty Talk with Men

Dirty talking with men doesn't actually have to be as intimidating as you may think that it will be. You can follow a few simple steps and figure out how to start talking to your own partner, no pressure involved. All you have to do is know what it is that you want to say, how you will say it, and how to keep it calm and natural. If you can do that, you will find that everything else is simple. You just have to work hard to give your partner that basic level of attention that will help him to feel like he is wanted, and he will be ready to go.

Start Small

Of course, you should always start small. When it comes to dirty talk, it can take a bit of time to get into that learning curve. For some, it is nearly instantaneous, but for others, it is highly difficult to get into the swing of things right away. You need to get to know each other, especially if you are in a new relationship. You need to know that your partner is actually interested in what you are saying or wanting and that your partner is open and receptive to what you are saying. If you can do that, you will find that everything else will follow simply.

Begin in privacy

Likewise, it is usually wise to start in private with your partner rather than being bold enough to get on with it in public. Some people may love whispering those naughty little words into each other's ears, but don't do that without first letting your partner know that they should expect you to do just that by doing it in private before ever attempting it anywhere else. This gives you the chance to make sure that you're both on the same page.

Personalize it

When it comes time to begin, make sure that your dirty talk is personalized. Don't just use random sayings and phrases that are not really tailored to anything. If your partner does not enjoy being called daddy, for example, calling him daddy constantly would be a major problem. Rather than doing that, it is more important for you to figure out what he likes. Does he like being told how good he feels? Does he like being told that he's doing a good job? Does he want you to beg for him to do something or to tell him what you want? Figure out what works for him—you'll know when he seems to get even more eager to fuck than before.

Keep it natural

Finally, don't overthink things. Let things happen naturally and say what comes to mind rather than attempting to come up with the cleverest thing that you can think to say. Rather, you should take the time to just say what comes to mind and see how he responds. It's trial and error, and really, is it that embarrassing to say something to someone that you are sexually intimate with?

Phrases for Dirty Talk with Men

- What do you want me to do?
- How do you want me?

- Your lips feel so good.
- Your [body part here is/are] so sexy
- I want you now.
- I want you to touch me here [guide his hand].
- I want you to fill me up right now.
- Cum in me.
- Fuck me harder.
- I want to do [name what you want] to you.
- I love your kisses.
- Your cock feels so good.

Tips for Dirty Talk for Men

Talk about it before you actually do the deed

This makes it so that you are both currently aroused and therefore are more likely to actually get somewhere with the conversation. Ask about what he wants to hear you say or how far he wants you to go.

Enjoy it in the heat of the moment

Spend time engaging in it whenever you can, and don't be ashamed when it comes to taking the time to enjoy it yourself. It is just as much for you as it is for him; make sure that you are paying attention to what is happening and how much fun you are having.

Pay attention to his reactions

Make sure that in the moment, when you are using dirty talk, you pay attention to what it is that his body language says. Many people do not want to admit when someone has crossed a boundary, especially during sex, but that is more important than ever to stop and point out the problem. If it looks like your partner is uncomfortable with an exchange, remember that.

Check in after the fact

When you are done with the sex itself, it is time for you to spend some time actually talking about what he thought. The act of checking in might serve as extra dirty talk and may turn him on even more. While they don't typically admit it, men are just as emotional as other people.

Take it outside of the bedroom

Your man will probably love a message every now and then telling him just how hot you're getting thinking about what he did the night prior or how much you enjoyed it in the moment. Take that time and capitalize on it.

Don't get discouraged

There is a good chance that sometimes, you will mess it up. Sometimes, you need to practice. It might be awkward at first. It might feel weird to say these things out loud, but it is so important to remember to remain persistent and to keep on trying. If you can have sex with this person, they probably won't judge you for saying something that misses the mark.

Reach out and tell him your current fantasy

Whether you are together or apart, you can tell your partner what it is that you are fantasizing about at that moment. Are you thinking about how much you want his mouth on yours or how much you want to feel his dick in you? Tell him that.

Narrate your enjoyment for him

When you are fucking, men want to hear your interpretation of what is going on. Let him know all about what it is that you are enjoying in the moment.

Invite him somewhere

Especially if you are at an event or something, you can whisper to him that you are going to go into an isolated area and waiting for him. This is a major turn on for most men, and he will love it.

Say things that are meant to be tempting

At random, you can drop something that you know will drive him crazy. Tell him that you're not wearing any underwear or that you've been peeling particularly turned on at that moment. Tell him all about that new wax that you got, or that you have something new in an intimate area that you want to show him.

Mind the voice

If you are talking to him, make sure that you use the best, breathiest voice that you can manage to entice him. Men love that breathy, quiet voice.

Tell him what you appreciate

Tell your man all about what he did last time that was entirely unbelievable to him. When you do this, you will not only turn him on when he realizes that something that he was doing was that great to you, he will also then be thinking all about what he did—further turning him on.

Wake him up with a sexy promise

You can also start by waking your man up in the morning and telling him all about what you will do to him that day at some point. Tell him all about what it is that you want to do to him so that you will be able to drive him wild. You could tell him that you had a sexy dream about him that you're going to reenact that night, for example, as you run your hand up and down his thigh, or you can tell him that you're going to blow him or fuck him or do something else that drives him insane.

Tell him when you're cumming

In the moment, tell him that you're getting close, and as you do finish up, let him know that you are. As annoying as it can seem in porn to some men, they actually find that hearing that they are bringing their partner to orgasm is actually incredibly sexy. So many people say that they are turned on knowing that their partner is turned on, and that is highly impressive for them.

Beg him not to stop in the moment

When you are having sex, make sure that when they are getting the angle or spot just right that you tell him that he is. Tell him how much he is driving you insane and let yourself enjoy it as well. It can seem weird at first to tell someone that you like it right there or like that, but men love the encouragement.

Tell him that you want to do that again

There is nothing more flattering than telling your partner that you want to do exactly that all over again. After all, most people won't bother trying to repeat their sex with people if it is not worth every single moment of it.

Ask for exactly what it is that you want in the moment

You can beg for him to do something else, or you can ask him to, and he will know that you are enjoying yourself and the moment enough to want to keep going and ask for what you want.

Or demand what you want

You can also demand exactly what you want from him as well. Some men are turned on by a take-charge partner, even when they are traditionally dominant, and he may respond well to you telling him that you want him to take you from behind, or to ride him or anything else.

Tell him to take you

When you give him your best fuck me eyes and tell him that you are his for the taking, he is going to be turned on almost immediately. It is sexy to tell someone that you want to be completely taken by them. It is almost like a gift, so to speak, with you offering up your body completely to someone else.

Ask to be used

Sometimes, the best sex is that which is completely without regard to standard expectations. You may not want to be used in your relationship, but there can be something about surrendering in the moment, and men can enjoy that.

Be yourself

Unless you've agreed to roleplay or something else, make sure that, at the heart of your dirty talk, you are still yourself. Don't say things that you don't actually want to say just for him. It is important that you are not forcing things and that you are following your own style. While you may never want to tell your partner to fuck your brains out and choke you (which some people may want), you might find that complimenting him as he fucks you to be your style, and that's okay too. Make it authentic and be yourself.

Ask if you can do something sexy

Sometimes just stopping and asking him for permission to do something for him can be a bigger turn on than just doing it yourself without waiting to hear if he wants to.

Tell him that you can't think about anything but his cock

Men love to know that you have them and their fucking, on the mind, and if you can tell him that all that matters to you in that moment is thinking about fucking them, you will turn them on in an instant.

Tell him that you're touching yourself while thinking about him

What is sexier than knowing that your partner is fantasizing about you while touching themselves? He will love to hear this.

Tell him to cum for you, or even in you

Make sure that you tell him that you want him to cum for you when you are ready, or you could even offer to let him cum in you. Men love being told that, and it can instantly escalate the situation.

Tell him to look at you

Eye contact can absolutely escalate the situation and make your partner go crazy for you, especially during the most intense moments.

Say his name

Men love to hear their names said out loud to them. Yelling, whispering, moaning, it all depends upon the individual man, but they generally love to hear it said. Just make sure that you don't accidentally use the wrong name.

Tell him how good the sex is

Men want to be validated, and you can do that by telling him just how well he's doing. Men love to hear all about how satisfied they are making you, and if you tell him just how much you're enjoying the moment, you will encourage him to go more and harder.

Give him carte blanche to tell you to do whatever he wants

Try spending a session giving your partner the authority to make any decisions that he wants. If he asks you to do something, give it a shot.

Let him know that on that day, he is free to do what he wants to enjoy himself.

Pay attention to pacing

When you are speaking to your partner, you should make sure that you get the pacing right. Early on in the encounter, or during the foreplay stage, you will probably speak to each other slowly and breathily. But, as things get heated, you will probably find that your breathing has picked up and that you are likely to speak quicker.

Chapter 4: Dirty Talk for Women

Women are a bit different than men in terms of what they want to hear. While at the heart of things, they want the same thing, to feel wanted, and to feel sexy, they also do not always want to be treated like a sex object. Yes, there are plenty of women who get off on being called a slut or a whore. Yes, there are plenty of women that want you to tell them what to do or rough them up, but there are also women who prefer more subtlety in their bed.

You need to learn to approach women the right way if you want to be able to properly turn them on, and thankfully, you have this chapter. Forego any notion that your woman wants to be called a dirty slut or that she wants you to destroy her sloppy pussy. She might but let her tell you that she wants you to do that before trying to establish it yourself.

The Right Approach

When it comes to fucking and dirty talk, you need to approach it the right way if you hope to turn her on the right way. The way that you approach her or talk to her will determine if she wants to actually get down to business with you or not. If you want to make sure that you are turning her on, you need to take the right approach in the first place. This means that you must remember that really when you're not turned on, dirty talk honestly sounds a bit ridiculous. It does, and that's okay! Think about it—the act of sex itself is honestly a bit ridiculous on its own. How weird is it that sex itself is just the act of rubbing your body against someone else's because you like the feeling? From a practical or logical position, just the act of sex is strange, so is it that hard to believe that narrating out that sex would also be strange?

However, you must make sure that you take the right perspective when you are speaking to women. You should make sure that you are subtle and only as raunchy or dirty as she is comfortable with. After all, dirty talk is meant to be something that everyone is comfortable with. You must make sure that your partner is just as comfortable and happy with what is happening as you are.

There are some words that are off limits as well—don't call her bits a vagina or even a cunt, unless she wants you to. You don't need to be so formal, nor do you need to be so vulgar, especially early on. Rather, make sure that you are making use of words that you know are generally accepted. Pussy, clit, boobs, and tits will do just fine.

Talk and Touch

The most effective dirty talk is able to combine talk and touch to make the most erotic setting possible so that she will enjoy every moment of what is happening to make a sensual, sexy moment that she will love. Mix erogenous zones, the areas on the body that are particularly sensual and create sexual pleasure. Turning someone on is not limited to just being in someone else's pants—all sorts of areas throughout the body are highly sensitive, and they can create that arousal that you are looking for. Women have several different areas in the body that are likely to be delightfully stimulating, including:

- **The clitoris:** This is the most sensitive of the erogenous zones, and if you want to turn someone on and get her off, the best place to focus on is her clit. Women love the pressure and the vibrations that can be used here.
- **The vagina:** The inside of the vagina is full of nerve endings, and deep stimulation is incredibly pleasurable. However, on the outside, lighter touches tend to be preferred.
- **The cervix:** This is the bottom of the uterus and is full of its own nerve pathways that can aid a woman in reaching orgasm.
- **The mouth and lips:** Kissing is essential to a relationship, but it also aids greatly in arousal. If you want to turn your partner on, you should make sure that you are willing and ready to play with both her mouth and her lips to really get her moving.

- **The neck:** The nape of a woman's neck is highly erotic for most women, especially with a light, gentle touch. If you want to turn her on, gently kiss at or nibble at her neck.
- **The nipples:** Nipples, when stimulated, turn on the same parts of the brain responsible for processing the clitoris and vagina. If you want to turn her on, nipple stimulation, particularly with pressure and vibrations, is a surefire way to do so.
- **The ears:** The ears on women are highly sensitive to touch, thanks to all of the nerve endings. This means that gently brushing over her ears while whispering your dirty talk into them is a fantastic way to turn her on and get her moving.

What She Wants to Hear

Women love to hear their partners making sounds. Silence says that you are not actually enjoying it at all, whether you are or not. Do your partner a favor and actually tell her what you are enjoying in the moment. Women want to hear something—*anything*—during sex, so long as you are not being offensive. Sound like you enjoy yourself, whether you are turning on the dirty talk or even just moaning or sounding like you are enjoying it. Tell her how much you like the sex or how hot she looks. Let her know how much you want to keep going or how you want her to continue. Really, so long as you are giving her positive feedback and you are making sure that you follow her boundaries, you are likely to get some pretty good feedback from her as well. She wants to know that she can feel wanted and desired. She wants to feel like you are having a good time.

Really, just about anything can be sexy if you know what you are doing and how you are talking to her. Follow her cues. Make sure that you are mindful of what she seems comfortable with as well, and don't lose sight that you are talking to her to turn her on, not for yourself. If you can do that, you are likely to have far more luck.

Phrases for Dirty Talk with Women

- You are so fucking gorgeous
- I love what you are doing with your [hand, mouth, pussy, etc.]
- How does that feel?
- I'm going to fill you up
- I want you so bad
- Cum for me
- I'm going to take you
- Your pussy feels so tight right now
- You taste good
- Do you like that?

- I need you right now

Dirty Talk During Foreplay

During foreplay, you have the benefit of being able to talk to her and turn her on. Much like men, she wants to hear you talk about what you want to do or what you *need* to do. Urgency is hot, and women want to hear that from you. If you can make it clear to her that you need her right that moment, you are going to get her wet. You can tell her that you want to do something to her with that urgent, quiet tone, and she will either oblige or ask you to do something else instead.

If you tell her that you are ready to fuck her, or you are able to tell her things that you want to do, you can get her ready in advance. You create that anticipation; you are fostering that sexual tension that will ensure that the big moment will be even better. Remember, women don't want to fuck someone that is disinterested. They want to be wanted, just like men do. They want to feel like they are desired and attractive. They want to feel like their partner is having a good time so that they are able to have a good time, and the sooner that you can make that good time happen, the better. You just have to know what you are doing and how to do it.

During foreplay, try telling her what you intend to do or what you wish that you could do. It will turn her on, and she may even follow through with it if you tell her that you want it enough. If you want to make sure that she's hot for you, you need to make sure that you make her believe that you want her first. There is not much that is hotter than being wanted in the first place.

Dirty Talk During Sex

During sex, things aren't much different—you want to make sure that you are talking to your partner and telling her just how much that you actually want her. Make her believe that you do genuinely want to enjoy her body and let her know how good she feels. Boost her confidence. Tell her that you are so happy with how she is feeling around you as you thrust into her so that she knows that you are enjoying it. Moan a bit. Let her hear just how much you enjoy it.

In the moment, women want to hear that they are good in bed. They want to feel like they are actually bringing you pleasure so that they can enjoy that pleasure as well, and the best way to ensure that that can happen is if you tell them. Of course, you want to tow that line carefully and make sure that what you are doing is something that they are comfortable with. You should always be willing to listen if someone says that something bothers them and make sure that you correct yourself if you continue to try to use that language in the future as well.

Tips for Dirty Talk for Women

Be tactful

Make sure that when you are using dirty talk, you do so tactfully. Make sure that you use it in situations that make sense or that call for it. This means that if you are having a serious conversation about something, you don't tell her that you wish that your hands were on her tits instead of listening to her.

Tell her when you're cumming

Women want to know when you're about to finish. Especially if they are on top, they don't want to continue bouncing away after you're done. Let them know when you're done so that they can accommodate.

Say her name

Just like with men, women want to hear their partners say their name. It is validating, and that acknowledgment brings great pleasure. It can elevate the eroticism of your sex and make it so much better just by dropping her name in there somewhere. Whether you mention her name, or you quietly moan her name to her as she rides you, making sure that you use her name is a great way to make her feel validated.

Sound like you are enjoying it

Make sure that when you are fucking, you sound like you are actually, well, fucking. Your silence is usually taken as being distracted or uninterested. It is far better for everyone involved if you sound like you genuinely enjoy it. Don't be embarrassed by any sounds that you might make—she'll find them attractive and enjoyable.

Tell her she's good in bed

When you tell her that she's good in bed, she'll feel validated and confident enough to want to continue fucking or to want to fuck in the first place. If you tell her how much you're looking forward to having sex and you specify why, you will find that you give her that much-needed confidence boost that will take you far.

Tell her in the moment what she is doing that you like

If she suddenly does something that is particularly enjoyable, such as using her tongue a certain way or touching you or kissing you a specific way, you can tell her that you like it. If you like it, tell her so she can do it again. She will find more enjoyment in the fact that you have complimented her as well.

Check in with her during sex

Ask her if she likes what you are doing, or if she needs you to do something else. See if there are ways that you can change what you are doing to make sure that you are tending to her every need as well. She will also feel more attracted to you when you clearly make it a point to check in with her to make sure that she is enjoying things.

Ask her what she wants you to do to finish her off

When it comes to it, you should make sure that you ask her what she wants, especially to get off with. You want to make sure that you satisfy her completely, and that means that you need communication. When you can feel that she's getting close, you can ask her what she wants you to do to finish her off. Sometimes, it is just that act of caring for her that can make her crave to be with you even more.

Set boundaries

If you are going to be sexual with someone else, make sure that you tell her that she can set a boundary without question. You can tell her that if she is uncomfortable with something, she should tell you. You want to make sure that she is able to tell you when you do cross a boundary. This makes her feel safe, and when she is safe and comfortable, she is going to be willing to unleash the sexual individual within her. If she feels like she is comfortable with you, she will feel like she can continue to be intimate with you and that she can push those boundaries and experiment with you, knowing that she can stop you if she ever feels uncomfortable.

Tell her she smells good

Let's face it—sex is kind of gross if you think about it. There are exchanges of fluids. You are kissing and in each other's faces. You are breathing on each other and getting sweaty as you fuck. She may be feeling a bit self-conscious during the act, but if you tell her that you love the way that she smells, you are letting her know that she is not gross. You are letting her know that she is attractive to you, and that will help her to unwind a bit and enjoy the moment more.

Tell her she's sexy

It can help greatly to tell her just how attractive and sexy that she is. Let her know how much you love to fuck her so that she can feel like she is confident enough to keep moving forward and to keep engaging with you.

Tell her you want to continue all night long

You can also make sure that you tell her that you want to continue your romp all night long to make her feel like she is the most important thing to you. You are effectively convincing her that she is your utmost priority and that above all else, you want her. You tell her that she is not competing against video games, friends, drinking, or anything else—you want her and her alone, and that is erotic.

Tell her to talk dirty to you

If you tell her to dirty talk with you, you will help inspire her further. You can get her to engage more with you when you do this, and that is a major turn on as well. Use this to really get her involved and to make her go crazy. After all, sex is a two-way street—you both have to be involved and engaged if you want the best possible sex.

Follow this pattern

Dirty talk doesn't have to be crass or aggressive—it can be affectionate with a long-term partner or a spouse as well. You can follow this simple strategy to make sure that you are giving the best possible dirty talk that you can: "It feels amazing when you [action] my [body part]" or "Your [body part] is so amazing, I want to [action] them." If you can follow this pattern, you will be able to compliment more than just her sex—you compliment her as a whole, and that is incredibly validating.

Be urgent

Very little is more of a turn on than being needed by someone. If you want to make someone want you, you make it clear that you *need* them. This works with women as well. Urgency is hot. If you want to make her wet, let her know how much you need her. Your voice should be almost a plea—like you need her more than anything else.

Tell her she tastes good

If you are going down on her, let her know that you like how her pussy tastes. It makes her feel like you want to be down in her pussy, pleasing her.

Moan

If you want her, tell her without needing to say a word. As you play with her, let her know just how badly you need her without a single word. Just a well-placed moan can say it all.

Tell her how hard/wet you are

If you have a penis, tell her how hard it is for her. If you have a vagina, tell her how dripping wet it is for her. She will love to hear how your body is working for her and how she is impacting the way that you are able to move and interact. She wants to know that she is ultimately

Comment on how wet she is

As you play with her, you can make mention of just how wet she is and how that makes you feel as well. You can tell her just how hot you think it is that she is as wet as she is so that she can feel a bit more confident about herself as well. Tell her just how enjoyable you find it.

Comment on how tight she is

Whether she is tight around your finger or your cock, let her know. Tell her just how much you like the feeling and how much you want to enjoy it. Comment on the feeling that you have around you and how great it is.

Tell her which position you want her in and what you are about to do to her

When you take charge like this, you will probably set her on fire. Most people enjoy being wanted so desperately that the other person is demanding that they do something. Of course, you must make sure that you are still respecting any boundaries that ought to be respected but let her know what you want.

Tell her how much you want her

Doting on her in the moment, saying just how badly you want her pussy around you, or to taste her on your lips, is going to set her off. It is highly erotic to be the object of someone's sexual attention, especially if there is a mutual attraction there.

Tell her how beautiful she looks in that position

Whether it is from behind, from above, or below, tell her just how great she looks to you in the moment as you are fucking her. She will eat it up.

Experiment until you find what you both like

Take some time to figure out what it is that you both want out of your relationship. Every now and then, in the moment, try something new and see if she responds well to it. She may love what you are doing, or she may wish that you would not do that ever again. Either way, you can get to know each other and what you both want better over time.

Tease her

All day long, tell her how much you want to enjoy her. Make her want you and let that tension build all day long. There is nothing better than making sure that the sexual tension is running high so that you will be able to take advantage of all of that pent up energy later on.

Tell her not to do something because it's turning you on

This goes right back to teasing. If she's walking around the store with you, you can lean over and whisper in her ears that if she keeps walking like that, you're going to have to do something about it at home because she's driving you wild. Of course, she'll then most likely do it more to drive you crazy too.

Tell her that you want to dominate her/have her dominate you

Depending upon the perspective that you take, you can either make her in charge, or you can choose to dominate over her. There is something about being in complete control, or alternatively, to giving someone else complete control, that can be a great turn on, especially when you and your partner are on the same page.

Tell her to scream for you

If you feel like she's getting a bit too lost in the moment, you can escalate by asking her to get loud for you, encouraging her to scream for you. Of course, you should be mindful of neighbors with this method.

Make her think about you by talking about how turned on she makes you

Even if you are not actively having sex in the moment, you can tell her all about how distracted you get when you think about her. She'll then be thinking about you thinking about her.

Tell her just how intoxicating you find her

Women love being doted on, and especially if you are trying to warm her up without just getting everything flowing right that moment, you can try telling her something about how enticing and intoxicating she is. Tell her the smell of her hair is mind-blowing, or that she looks absolutely divine and that you can't keep your eyes off of her. Tell her just how attracted you are to her and that you can't stop looking/smelling/thinking about her.

Chapter 5: Digital Dirty Talk

We live in a digital age—there is no way around it. That means that you need to stop and consider that you are no longer stuck talking to each other. You don't just have to talk to each other in person anymore. You have the internet in the pocket of your pants these days—you have an ability to communicate at will if you want it. All you have to do is pull it out of your pocket and use it. That's right, your phone is the greatest facilitator of foreplay and sexing when it comes to turning on your partner with ease. All you need to do is make sure that you know how to write the best sext you can. As you read here, we are going to be looking at how to sext, how to pace things, and how to overcome the initial awkwardness of what you are doing. We will also talk about the importance of being able to take a picture that is enticing but not too revealing, as well as several tips to help you.

How to Sext

Sexting makes one of the greatest forms of foreplay, which you can use just about anywhere at any time. So long as you are mindful of your phone, you can simply send messages back and forth all day long, building up that anticipation and making sure that both you and your partner are driving each other wild. You can tell them all of the fantasies that you have throughout your time. You can tell your partner what you want them to do, or what you want to do to them. You can make sure that you are taking the time to drive them insane as well. When you play your cards right, you can keep that sex desire on their mind all day long, and that means that when you finally are able to come together again, you can enjoy all of that passion again.

Sexting does not have to be difficult or challenging. However, there are a few considerations to keep in mind. You want to make sure that you follow a few rules so that you avoid running into other problems.

Mind the timing

Make sure that you are well aware of what your partner's schedule looks like so you do not send them a message when they are in a place where it would be considered inappropriate. While technically just about any time would be inappropriate, it is important to keep in mind that your partner may be busy at work when you sext them, or they may be with family or other people that should not be exposed to that. Rather than just sending a sexy picture, try coming up with a code word. Ask your partner if they are busy before you do anything at all.

Be slow

Make sure that when you are sexting your partner, you mind the fact that your conversation should move slowly. You don't want to just go from 0 to 60 in an instant—rather, you want to make sure that you start slow and that you want to play. Talk about how much you enjoyed the other night or send a subtly suggestive picture.

Stay within your comfort zone

Make sure that, no matter what, you work within your comfort zone. Your sexting doesn't need to be explicit—you can even just send a message saying that you're ready to have fun with your partner, or you can send pictures of yourself masturbating if you really wanted to. You should start slowly and make sure that you are comfortable with where the sexting is going at any point in time.

Always send a warning before nudes

If you are going to send a picture that's not safe for work, give them that warning. You don't want them to get in trouble at work if your nude popped up on their lock screen, nor do you want them to open the message with others around or within sight of your picture.

Have fun

Remember, the whole point of dirty talk and sexting is to have fun and to encourage that sexual tension that will help you to really enjoy the moment. This means that you should enjoy the entire time that you are sexting. You can even draw your inspiration from porn, erotica, and romance novels.

Details matter

When you are sexting, the details are where the bulk of your content is. You need to make sure that you are actively encouraging each other to provide yourselves with the right amount of details. If you can nail that, you will be just fine.

Pacing for Good Digital Dirty Talk

Just like with sex, good digital dirty talk and sexting needs to be just the right pacing, or you are going to run into all sorts of problems. If you want to make sure that you are able to turn your partner on without anything else happening, you want to make sure that you understand the right pacing. You should always start slow at first and build up. When you are just getting started, you should make sure that you lead into it. Talk about how much you miss the other person or that you're thinking of them. Send a few suggestive emojis or a picture that is suggestive, but not revealing.

Think of good digital dirty talk as being quite like sex—you build up to the big moment. You talk about fucking each other and about enjoying it. You go over what it is that you want from each other, enacting fantasies. Think of the following exchange:

I'm thinking of you.

Really? I was thinking about the other night just now. I really liked what you did with your tongue.

Mmm, yeah, I'd like to do that again. I want to kiss and tease you up until you're shaking and begging for more.

Yes, please. I want to feel you tonight.

I can come over and then we can cum over together ;)

Notice how it is not particularly explicit right off the bat. It's teasing, light, and suggestive. It is not meant to be highly explicit at first. It is something that is supposed to build up that tension so that when you are together, you have enough of that tension built up that you can't keep your hands off of each other. Whether you are sexting as your own personal porn as you masturbate or if you are sexting just to build up that tension, you are making sure that you and your partner are ready to go.

Overcoming Awkwardness of Digital Dirty Talk

Sexting can be a bit awkward if you don't know what you are doing, but don't let that deter you. Too many people think, "Wow, I'm not creative enough for this, or I can't think of anything to say." However, that doesn't mean that you can't enjoy it. Sexting can be great. It can be fun and playful while also being erotic. You don't have to start out too explicitly, nor do you ever have to go further than you want to. Start out slowly and work your way up to what you want. If getting a text that says, "This is waiting for you," and a picture of a hard cock is a turn off for you, say something. Make it clear that that is not working for you.

The best way to overcome the awkwardness is honestly just to get started and make it happen. Even if for you it is a compliment or a vague reference to that last time that you and your partner did something highly erotic, that is still something. Even a message as innocent as "I miss your lips on mine," can be erotic. It tells them what you want in that moment and is also an invitation for your partner to take control.

You can also ask questions that can lead to the fantasies and sexually explicit messages that you want. Ask your partner what they are thinking about in the moment to open up the conversation. Ask them what their fantasy is and let them take control. This can eliminate some of the awkwardness for yourself as well.

Consider these different options to start up your conversation with your partner that are able to skip that initial awkwardness:

- I want you to keep me warm
- I'm thinking about you
- What are you up to right now?
- Your lips on my [body part] feel so great
- I miss your hands on my [body part]
- When's the last time you thought about me?
- I'm getting wet/hard thinking about you right now
- Want to try something new tonight?

Taking the Perfect Picture

Taking the perfect picture is important to your sexting life, and the best ways that you can make that happen typically involve having some fun and finding just the right angles. Keep in mind that when you take your pictures, a lot of the time, less is more. When you are trying to choose the right photo, try taking several and looking through them until you can find the right angles for you. Every person has their own angles that make them look amazing—it is just a matter of figuring out where they are.

Start by making sure that you know your angles. This is one time where selfie sticks can be your greatest asset. Make sure that you experiment regularly and that you remember that natural lighting can be a great asset as well. Your pictures do not have to be revealing. They do not have to be anything other than suggestive. You could post a picture of your thighs without taking off your skirt. You could show your cleavage without revealing any nipple. If you are a man, you could show some abs or a toned arm without ever taking off your pants.

You can also work by making your phone your partner. Instead of trying to take a photo just right, you can focus on the image as if your phone itself is your partner, engaging in what is effectively POV pictures that will create that image of your partner being your phone. You will put your picture in the position that you would prefer your partner and then get into the right position, looking right at the camera.

With the right angles and the right attitude, you can usually figure out exactly what it is that you should be doing. Take a whole bunch of pictures and then make sure that the ones that you choose are the right angles and that they make you look great. If you can do that, you will find that you can take the sexiest pictures with ease.

What Not to Do during Sexting

Of course, if you are sexting, there are a few things that you should absolutely avoid at all costs to make sure that ultimately, you are doing the right thing at the right time. Make sure that you keep the following in mind so that you avoid common mistakes that can be problematic.

- **Don't send unwanted photos:** Regardless of whether you are a man or a woman, avoid the unsolicited nudes, especially if you haven't told them that you intend to send any.
- **Don't send photos to someone that you can't trust:** If you have just started dating someone or you can't trust the person that you are dating, don'ts end them any photos.
- **Don't take things too seriously:** Remember, sexting is supposed to be fun. Don't take it too seriously and enjoy the time that you spend teasing your partner.

Tips for Digital Dirty Talk

Offer up something that you want to do

What's sexier than detailing out exactly what you intend to do with your partner? Send them a message with you telling them exactly what you will be doing the next time that you all get together.

Be detailed

Remember that in sexting, all of the details are what do the talking. In engaging with sex, you are able to lead with your body, but in sexting, you must lead with your words instead.

Talk about dreams

Spend some time telling your partner all about a dream that you just had so that your partner can understand just how much you like or are thinking about him or her.

Tell them that you're in the shower

This invites them to text you with all sorts of different things, from what they will do to you when they see you, just imagining you naked and fresh out of the shower.

Be honest

Tell them exactly what you've felt so that they have the opportunity to reciprocate if they want to. This can open up all sorts of fun sexting ideas, and all you have to do is tell them about what it is that you want.

Have your partner turn off image previews

Make sure that your partner is not going to have your sexy picture plastered on his screen in public areas where it could be embarrassing for both of you. If you intend to sext with each other, make sure that your images and messages will not be on display for the world to see at a glance.

Turn on the heat

You can tell them that you are fantasizing about them right there in the moment and ask what they think about what you are saying. This is a great way to turn them on and get them engaging with you.

Express your regret that they're not there with you

This is a great way for you to tell them that you are disappointed that, at the end of the day, they are not present with you. This could take the place of saying something along the lines of, "Man, I wish you were here," to "It's too bad that you're not here right now."

Ask them to guess what you are thinking about

You should also try asking them what they think that is on your mind right at that moment. From being excited about how you are thinking about them, to all of the fun you intend to have encouraged, to guess what is on your mind, and then share whether they are right or not.

Let them know what you are wearing

Or not wearing. Tell them what you have on and ask what they want to do with you. They will probably want to tantalizingly remove each and every item that you are wearing

Ask them to take you

Because you will be in a position where you can say just about anything, try asking them to take you. You would be surprised at the results that you get when they think that all you want is a good, hard fuck, especially if that is you telling them the truth.

Only send messages that you feel comfortable sharing

Unfortunately, a few bad apples tend to ruin things for everyone, and sexting is yet another example of exactly that. Too many people have been burned by trying to sext, only to have their images plastered up online or disbursed among people. This is a major problem, and you want to nip it in the bud so that it cannot be a problem. Don't let anyone pressure you into sending messages that you don't want to send.

Tempt them with previews

Give them a quick sneak peek of everything that you intend to do to them as soon as they get home or to your place. If you intend to drop his pants as soon as he walks in the door and you tell him that, make sure that you are willing to follow through with it.

Play with the senses

Sure, you're apart, but that doesn't mean that you have to ignore the sense of touch, taste, or smell. You can entice each and every sense with the words that you type onto your phone and send off to him or her, and there is a good chance that using those words will drive him insane.

Make a request

These requests can be kind or demanding—you can ask politely for something, or you can tell them that you need them right that moment and that you can't wait any longer to get your hands on them.

Tease them
Tell them vaguely what you are doing or thinking about, only to make them wait a bit before you respond. This will drive them crazy, wondering what they are going to get back from you.

Send a quick video for them

If you are feeling especially brave, send a quick message with a video showing what you are doing to yourself. It could be a quick preview of you masturbating, or even your big O moment to drive the other person wild.

Reminisce about sex that was amazing

Tell them something that they did that you are thinking about at that moment. Talk about how much you miss that moment and what it made you think or feel.

Compliment them

Tell them what they did that you really enjoyed recently and just how much it impressed you. By sending compliments sometimes, you can usually get your partner to start thinking about that time, which of course, is a turn on.

Thank them for something

Sometimes, what they have done is so memorable to you that you need to send them a quick thank you message. Telling them that you appreciate what they have done sexually is a great way to validate them and turn them on quicker.

Come up with your responses for when you're not sure what to say back

Sometimes, you will get a message that you're unsure about how you should respond. When that happens, try saying something like, "wow, that turns me on so much," or "Tell me more." When you encourage them to keep talking, you are engaging even if you don't know what you should be saying back.

Have a roleplay session

You can sext a roleplay. You can write out what you are doing, in your mind, of course, and the other party can reply to you with what they do in response. You might not be able to touch each other, but you can write out your fantasies with each other and imagine it all happening, driving each other insane as you do so.

Be adventurous

Make sure that when you are talking to your partner, you are adventurous. If there was ever a time to pursue and explore your sexuality, it would be during the time in which you are able to engage digitally without any pressure of following through physically. If you discover that you don't like it, then you don't like it, and that's that.

Send pictures

Even if you just send something suggestive, go for it and see what happens, especially if you've talked about doing so in the past. People are visual creatures, and it can be highly erotic to see the impact that you have on someone else's body when they're not expecting it.

Get creative with the language

Make sure that when you are messaging him, you keep in mind that you can only say cock and pussy so much before it is time to change things up. Try to get creative, or even poetic sometimes. You might find that somethings that strikes them the right way and gets them to do what you want more than anything else.

Remember it's a conversation

When you are sexting someone, remember that it is a two-way conversation. You should be paying attention to the way that you engage with the other person and let him or her have some fun getting to talk. Remember that you should both be engaging with each other rather than anything else.

Use sexting as a precursor to dirty talk

Dirty talk in person can be quite awkward, but ultimately, it can be a great way for you to practice talking about what you want and a great exercise in communication that will help to ensure that you are able to talk in the moment as well. You can tell them exactly what you want—tell them that you want them to suck you off or tease you or fuck you via text and, eventually, work up to saying it in person as well.

Be ready to take it live

At some point, be ready to take what is being said live. Your sext session may very quickly turn into wanting to actually video chat or even meet up quickly to see what is going on.

Check in afterward

After sex, you have the ability to cuddle with each other or spoon or enjoy the moment. That is not quite so easy to do when you are engaging in sexting just due to the fact that you aren't close enough. However, you can take the time to check in with the other person and make sure that they recognize that they should be mindful of how they are interacting.

Ask your partner what turns them on

This is a great way to get them thinking about what it is that you can do for them, which not only helps you to know how to address a sexting session but will also ensure that you are able to address those needs in person as well.

Ask what they like you to do or like about you

You want to make sure that you are involving your partner and letting them choose what it is that turns them on. Have them tell you what it is about you that drives them crazy.

Chapter 6: What NOT to Do

Of course, when it comes to dirty talk and sexting, it is important that you pay attention to some pretty important things that should never be done. As you read through this chapter, you are going to be introduced to several things that you should just never do when you are using dirty talk. Make sure that you communicate what it is that you want to do and how you can make it happen as well. You want to make sure that when it comes right down to it, your partner knows what it is that will turn you on more than anything, but you also need to know what not to do.

If you go too far too quickly with dirty talk in general, you can cause some serious problems. You could, for example, completely ruin the sexual relationship entirely. You can destroy any trust that is had or any respect that is necessary for a mutually consensual relationship, and let's be honest here—no one wants to do that. For that reason, it is highly important for you to take the time to communicate what you want, boundaries, and understand what not to do.

This list will provide you with thirty things that you should *never* do in dirty talk. Of course, there will always be the occasional exception to the rule, but if you pay attention to what not to do, you can usually make sure that you and your partner are on the same page enough to ensure that neither of you are hurting the other.

Escalating too quickly

Remember that you can't go from 0 to 60 without first stopping and asking what the other person wants. If it is your first encounter with this person, don't start it off by calling her a dirty little slut with a pussy that needs to be punished for being so sloppy. You could *try* to do that, but there is a very real, very good chance that doing so is going to create a major problem for you and your relationship. Instead, try focusing on what you can do to slowly bring up the heat of what you are saying to what you want it to be. Start slowly and avoid moving too quickly.

Not going far enough

On the other hand, if you are super sterile about what you are saying, you won't turn anyone on at all. You need to be able to follow that bridge between too much and not enough if you want to be able to convince your partner that you really do want him or her. If your voice is flat or you are not talking at all, you may tell the other person that you're just not interested, even if that is not actually the case at all.

Timing it wrong

Make sure that when you are reaching out or using dirty talk, your timing is right. If you are in the middle of a conversation with someone, don't suddenly completely change the mood, especially if the initial communication was there because of the way that you are feeling in the moment. You need to be able to understand that ultimately, there is a time and place for everything.

Not being believable

Make sure that when you talk to your partner, you make it believable. It is not believable to say that you've been jerking it for the last three hours when you are at work, for example, nor is it believable that you would walk around work for three hours pitching a tent. Make sure that whatever you say, you make it believable so that your partner is just as turned on as you are.

Making it seem rehearsed

You also should make sure that you avoid making any attempts to interact with your partner seem too rehearsed. You can't tell your partner the exact same line that you have rehearsed and repeated over and over again and hope that they will listen. If things seem too automatic, you have a very real chance of simply offending the other person rather than actually making any good, clear progress with what you are attempting to do. It is always more important to be honest and realistic than anything else.

Making it too complicated

Dirty talk doesn't have to be complicated, nor should it be. You need to make sure that any dirty talk that you are using is going to be effective and usable without having to worry too much about repercussions. When you are able to talk dirty to someone else, it should not be super complicated, nor should it be full of all sorts of attempts to make you seem smarter or try-hard than you actually would normally be.

Not personalizing it enough

Another common mistake that people make are making their dirty talk too impersonal. Yes, you can say the same thing to just about anyone, but are they all going to respond the same way? Are they all really going to appreciate the way that you have chosen to approach them? Many people find that they are far happier if they are able to have any dirty talk personalized. Instead of just saying, "Fuck me harder," you can figure out how to personalize it—"I love the way you're riding me with that thick cock of yours," for example. Now you are getting specific and personalizing, which allows for more connection and, therefore, more intimacy as well. You need to be able to keep that line just right between not enough and just enough.

Making your partner uncomfortable with it

You should always make sure that you are able to keep your partner comfortable during dirty talk, and this means that you and your partner must have some very serious talks about boundaries to make sure that you are both able to follow along and be comfortable. Of course, this also means that you both will need to be willing to talk about boundaries so that neither of you are unintentionally pushing things too far one way or another.

Repeating back what your partner has said

Even if your partner has just said the sexiest thing imaginable, there is no reason to repeat it back to them. Don't tell them exactly what they just said to you unless you want them to stop and look at you like you completely missed the point. Make sure that you are telling them things that are new and unique to make sure that they are able to understand that you are, in fact, attempting to turn them on, not to make a complete fool out of yourself as you go.

Any mention of pregnancy or making babies

Especially if you and your partner are not exclusive or are not long-term partners, you should leave out any talk of babies. If it is a casual fuck session with your booty call, you should not be telling them that you can't wait to put babies into them. No matter how hot it may seem in the moment, all you are doing is setting your partner up for expectations that are unreasonable and also making it a point to completely avoid the way that you should be interacting. Parenthood is not sexy. While some people revel in it, especially the first year, sex drives can tank, and when that happens, you don't want to be talking about putting a baby into someone else. Likewise, you should not tell your partner that you want them to put a baby in you, either.

Leave food out of it

Unless this is something that the two of you have discussed, don't refer to his or her bits as food objects. Most people don't find calling someone's penis a sausage particularly attractive. It is problematic for most people, in fact, and you can run into all sorts of issues if you are not mindful of the way that you approach the situation. Instead, just leave food where it belongs—in the kitchen and out of your bedroom life.

There is a time and place to be romantic and sweet

Keep in mind that there is absolutely a time for romance and being sweet—and that is rarely during active fucking. Recognize that there is a major difference between fucking, which is usually regarded as almost animalistic in the way that it is used and being willing to sensually make love to someone else. If you are fucking, don't whisper sweet nothings into your partner's ear. If you are making love, don't tell her that her pussy is so tight and wet. Know the difference between romantic sex and passion, no strings or emotions attached sex, and adjust accordingly.

Don't discuss bodily fluids

The only bodily fluids that have a place in your sex life are ejaculate and the lubricant that vaginas make. Don't tell your partner that you want to pee on them, especially if you are just starting out, and you don't know his or her kinks yet. You need to take the time to get to know them and make your actions accordingly. It is only then when you are careful about what you are doing that you can make that appropriate progress. Leave out urine, spit, and any other fluids unless explicitly discussed and agreed to in advance.

Leave the exes out of it

There is nothing worse than enjoying the moment only to suddenly be compared to an ex, whether being better or worse. No matter whether the comment is meant as a compliment or not, you do not want to think that your partner is busy comparing you to see how you stand up against your ex-boyfriend or girlfriend. That's a great way to set up all sorts of resentment and concern that things are going to go wrong if you are not careful. Instead, pay close attention to the ways that you engage with your partner and make sure that you are choosing to give them the respect that they deserve without worrying about the exes that are involved.

Don't make your dirty talk or sexting scenario too impossible

If you are sexting or dirty talking someone else, unless you have both agreed to do some roleplay, don't make your situation suddenly so fantastic that it will take away from the moment. This means don't suddenly be fucking your partner on another planet or something. Make it believable and call it good. This is one of the most important things that you can do to make sure that you are being effective with your small talk. You must make it believable and enjoyable.

Avoid making puns, no matter how tempting

It happens to the best of us at some point in time—that pun comes to mind, and it's really hard to resist saying it. However, keep in mind that when you are using puns with people, you keep those puns out of the bedroom. Most people won't find it attractive if you suddenly drop a pun off of something that you were enjoying just moments prior, and you can completely destroy the moment if you are not careful.

Make sure that you don't say something ridiculous

Similarly, try to avoid anything that is too ridiculous as you are fucking. This is not the time or place for that. Rather, this is the time and place for you to enjoy the moment. Avoid making any jokes at all during this period of time and try to keep your talking as serious as possible in the moment. Say things that are sexy. Don't say things that are going to be annoying, silly, or potentially kill the mood.

Listen to the suggestions that your partner makes

If your partner asks you to do something, you should do it. Make sure that you are regularly doing what your partner has requested of you so that you are able to figure out what it is that you need to do to get the most enjoyment for both of you. After all, if you want him to come back for seconds, or you want her to beg you for it, you are going to want to make sure that your sex is memorable enough for you to want to do it again. The best way to get that memorable nature is to make sure that you are doing whatever your partner has suggested.

Don't be too derogatory (at first)

Unless explicitly told that it is okay to call your partner's vagina a dirty, slutty cunt, you probably shouldn't do it. Especially if your relationship is still new and you are still getting to know each other, you do not want to unintentionally make things worse by saying the wrong things, and the easiest way to push too far is to use derogatory language that is going to turn everyone off from the situation. Rather than giving in to that derogatory language, you should instead consider having a genuine conversation about what it is that you and your partner both want.

Don't tell them to be quiet

If your partner is starting to moan or really enjoy the moment, one of the worst things that you can do is tell him or her to be quiet because they are distracting you. Instead of looking at their moans of pleasure as distractions, consider seeing them for what they are—clear signs that you are doing a good job because the other person literally cannot control the sounds that they are making in that moment. If you were to tell them to quiet down, all you would do is make them feel self-conscious or even make them feel like the relationship not worth continuing.

Don't try to convince the other party to skip the condom

All too often, you will hear men try to get out of wearing a condom during sex. However, that is not only bad practice because you can unintentionally end up pregnant, it is also dangerous if you are not in a committed relationship with someone that you trust. There is no place in dirty talk for risky, potentially dangerous sex, and because of that, do not even try to convince your partner that you do not need a condom. Newsflash—you *do* need a condom, and you *do* need to make sure that you are wearing it the right way.

Don't be too anatomically correct

While it is important to make sure that you are not being too vulgar, you also shouldn't overcorrect—do not tell her that you want to put your penis in between her labia and thrust into her vaginal cavity. That's not sexy. At all. Instead, make sure that you stick to generally acceptable terms. Cock and pussy, for example, are pretty regularly respected and acceptable.

However, terms like cunt are debatable for many and should be avoided unless she specifically tells you to call it a cunt.

Don't dwell on something that upsets the other party

If you make a mistake in the moment, it's okay—it happens to the best of us. However, unless you have seriously triggered your partner, you don't have to suddenly stop what you're doing. Rather, you can offer a quick apology and keep on moving forward unless your partner shows signs of wanting to stop. This means that there is no real reason for you to be rejecting everything that you're doing. There is no real reason for you to stop everything to suddenly apologize repeatedly and have a long, drawn out conversation, especially if the other party shows no desire to have one at that moment. You can revisit later if you really want to make sure that you have that conversation.

Don't ask if they are faking things

One of the worst things that you can do in the moment is to accuse your partner of faking something. Your partner should be trustworthy, and you should be able to feel like, if your partner is saying something to you, they mean it. Don't act like your partner is lying to you just because you think that they are being unrealistic. If you are worried about them being truthful, you probably shouldn't be pursuing that relationship in the first place.

Don't criticize your partner's bodies

It should go without saying that during sex or sexual play unless explicitly told otherwise, there is no real room for insulting the body of another person. Unless you have both discussed the idea of playing with degrading each other, there is a high likelihood that you are just going to upset each other and create all sorts of major problems. It is better to leave the degradation out of all dirty talk until you and your partner have had that candid discussion. While some people live by, it is better to ask forgiveness than permission; you can destroy your sexual relationship in this manner relatively simply. Don't even bother risking it—it isn't worth it.

Don't bring up dirty talk during a sensual, romantic sex session

Remember that sometimes, if your session is sensual and romantic, it is best to leave the dirty talk out of it—the aggressive kind, anyway. Rather, focus on the moment, and instead of degrading comments, you should be shifting into talk of how much you are enjoying yourselves, how much you care for each other, and how you enjoy the other person's body. Aggressive dirty talk has no place if you are attempting to woo someone else.

Don't call yourself daddy unless the other party has expressed an interest

Daddy is probably one of the more controversial names that you can call your partner during sex. Some people love it, and others hate it—you kind of have to go with the flow to make it work for you. If you want to be called daddy, then let your partner know and ask how she feels. Likewise, if you want to call him daddy, you should ask in advance. Some people find it a turn on, but others may find that it is a bit weird for them, especially if he already has children that refer to him as daddy. That can be something that is pushing the agenda too far and will get all sorts of backlash. Consider having a discussion about this prior to letting it be used. This is the best interest for everyone involved, and if you don't want to ruin the moment, you will ask first

Don't try to push boundaries when they have been set

While expressing desperation for sex can be hot, begging to do something that your partner has already said that they would not do is a huge turn off. Maybe she doesn't want to have anal sex—that's her right. You can ask her, but if she says no, it is best for you to drop the point altogether. However, if you start to push the point after you have already said no, you are making a big mistake. You will probably turn him or her off quicker than anything else if you continue to push a point that has already been answered. Remember, healthy sex is all about consent, and that consent must not be coerced.

Don't talk about family in bed

Finally, make sure that talks bout real life, such as family, friends, work, or anything else, are left out of the bedroom during sex. Nothing can turn off your dirty talk game quicker than mentioning that your mother is bothering you again. Instead, you should make sure that any interactions that you have with your partner are carefully crafted. Make sure that your interactions are focused on your partner rather than other concerns or problems that may be arising. Are those problems serious? Sure—but they also shouldn't be overwhelming so much so that you are unable or unwilling to have good sex because of them. Be all in or all out, but don't drag your partner down with talks of what your family is doing or why your job is currently driving you crazy.

Chapter 7: Bonus Tips to Spice Up the Bedroom

Congratulations! You've made it through the book and know now how you can begin to implement dirty talk. However, you may be wondering what else you can do to spice up your bedroom life now that you have a pretty solid idea of what to do and what not to do. Thankfully, you are in the right spot, and as you read through this chapter, you will be introduced to all sorts of information that is going to help you really spice up that sex life without much of a hassle at all. All you need to do is make sure that you know what you are doing and how to do it so that you can enjoy your bedroom and your partner. Now, let's take a look at some more tips that you can use to ensure that your bedroom life is never lacking what you are looking for.

Sexy daddy roleplay

Roleplay is a great way that you will be able to spice up your bedroom, and you can do it with dirty talk. You can talk to your partner about a way that you would like to explore. A common one is with daddy roleplay, where one person is the daddy, and the other is the daughter. You can make use of all sorts of dirty talk as you talk to each other, talking in a completely different context. It can really spice things up when you make use of new scenarios in which you and your partner are going to be able to make sure that you and your partner are able to get off together with that dirty talk. Talk to each other about your boundaries and see if that is something that you are interested in trying. It may not be for everyone, but some people love it.

Sexy delivery roleplay

Along a similar vein, a lot of people enjoy spicing things up with other roleplays as well. A common one is pretending to have your partner deliver a pizza. Maybe you have your partner go out to pick up your favorite pizza, and when he comes back home with it, he knocks on your door, and... you don't have any money! You can't find your cash and realize that you have no way to pay for it. However, with dirty talk and the power of being able to seduce your partner, because you happened to be nude with nothing but a robe on when your partner knocked, you are able to seduce him to pay it back.

As you have fun in this way, you can add in all sorts of dirty talk, making a game out of it that you can both get off to. He can call you his little slut for putting out for pizza, and you can rock his world by getting into a role that is completely different than the one that you typically lead. After all, he is not calling you a slut; he is calling the character the slut. You may also consider getting a bit rougher than usual as well, of course respecting any boundaries that have been requested so that you and your partner can both have the best possible time with each other.

Sexy teacher roleplay

Another roleplay idea that is ripe for the dirty talk is the idea of a teacher and a student. One of you can be the newbie virgin that has never had sex before, while the other is responsible for teaching the first one everything that he or she knows about having an awesome sex life. If you want to make sure that you and your partner get the most out of this exercise, introduce all sorts of dirty talk and molding one character to match what the other character is requesting. There can be all sorts of eroticism added in if you have one person pretending to be completely new to sex while the other then gets to do all of the leading. Not only do you set up for dominance there, but you also set up for other situations in which you are able to do so much more as well.

Sexy dirty talk boss and worker roleplay

One last roleplay suggestion is that you make use of a situation in which one of you is the boss, and the other is the secretary worker. You can use this as another position of power dirty talk roleplay. Of course, this is another situation where you can naturally find some ways that you will be able to make use of all sorts of dirty talk. You can have the secretary doing every single thing that the boss wants him or her to do. This is a great way that you are able to spice things up—after all, isn't having that control or power great sometimes?

Sexy storytime

Another way that you can really get each other off in the bedroom is to tell a dirty story as you touch the other person. Maybe one of you is jerking off the other as you tell a story to him. You can tell him all about what you want to do or about a fantasy that you have as you are slowly jerking him as foreplay. Make it full of all sorts of dirty talk as you do, and maybe even get into some rough interactions as well if you need to. It's a great way for you to be able to really get into what is going on. Likewise, you can switch off, so he plays with you while he tells you the dirty, sexy story as well. This is a great little switch off in which you are both able to get that fucking that you want, and you are both able to really turn each other on.

Narrate what the other person needs to do with themselves

You can also try adding in the dirty talk by having one of you tell the other person what you want them to do. You can tell your partner to masturbate your way, using all sorts of dirty talk. You could, for example, tell him that you want him to jerk his cock harder in your face with his balls dangling. You could tell her that you want to see her handle those big tits, pinching her nipples. You get a show out of telling and narrating what you want the other person to do. And because you are able to get that show out of it, you can really spice up that bedroom. It may not be typical to have yourself and your partner masturbating for each other, but it can be enjoyable in the moment. You can even do this over sexting as well to really up the ante and make things hotter.

Sexy narrated blow jobs

If your partner has a cock, this one is for you. You want to make sure that you are giving your partner exactly what he or she wants, and you can do that easily through making use of dirty talk that will blow both of your minds. You will be able to figure out exactly what matters the most in your relationship, and you will figure out how best to ensure that everyone is getting along the right way. All you have to do is make sure that you talk dirty as you suck on his cock.

When you are sucking on him, every now and then, you can moan as if you love every moment. Tell him how much you like to suck on it or how much you like to let your teeth run along it. Tell him to talk dirty to you or to grab your hair and guide you while he talks to you about what he wants.

This can go both ways as well. The woman can get licked and do the talking as well.

Blindfold and dirty talk narration

You can try adding in a blindfold to your relationship too, and if you really wanted to enjoy it, you would have the person who is not blindfolded narrating what he or she is about to do to the other person as it happens. As you do this, you encourage the other person to hear you out and build up sexual tension as well. This is a wonderful way that you will be able to enjoy every moment of that dirty talk as you fuck.

Think about it—what could be sexier than having someone else narrate how they are going to fuck you, just before they do it and when you can't see what they are doing? It can be highly erotic. You can even change things up by blindfolding him first and then taking him somewhere else that he doesn't expect.

Let him/her beg for sex as you deny it— for the time being

Another way to really build up that sexual tension is to tease and tease your partner, through dirty talk, through touch, and any other methods that you may choose to make use of. Perhaps you have a game to it—you are only willing to put out if they do something, but you don't tell them what that something is, and they spend the day trying to convince you what it will take. There are so many options for this—perhaps the magic solution is that you want them to say something in particular—perhaps you want them to literally beg for that sex. You would then use dirty talk to lead them to that particular answer. "How bad does that hot little pussy want me?" or "What will you do to get me to fuck you?" As you lead with all sorts of other dirty talk, you will probably find that your partner is willing to do a lot—and as soon as he or she begs, you then give in because that was what you had decided was going to be the cue.

Dirty talk teasing game

Most people know about the typical drinking games where everyone watches these movies together, and at certain points, there are shots taken. It could be that, for example, you take a shot when the main characters say something that is particularly cringe-worthy. However, have you ever played the dirty talk version? For this game, you and your partner will find some porn that the two of you can enjoy. You will then make a list of different actions that are worth different scores, so to speak. If you hear the woman in the video moan or whine, you may say that you are going to make out for thirty seconds, hands off. If you hear dirty talk in the video, you may have to say something yourself toward the other person and get them involved as well. Set up your scoreboard and let it go.

Dirty talk challenge

Another way that you can spice up the bedroom is by trying the dirty talk challenge. This will serve as foreplay all day long. You will effectively be tasked with messaging your partner all day long as much as is reasonable with your own dirty talk. The goal is that you have to keep his mind on you for most of the day. You want to make sure that he can't think about what he is supposed to be doing so that you can take advantage yourself. Make it as creative as you can and try to make sure that you keep him or her turned on as much as possible all day long.

Write a sexy letter

For partners that you are a bit closer to, you can let your creative juices flow, and hopefully, some erotic juices as well. Take some time to write a letter to your partner with all sorts of dirty talk. The idea is to have your partner turned on without touching him or her once—just by creating the letter and handing it off to them. If you can do this, you will be able to make him, or her want you at will. You will spice up your bedroom by adding in an instant turn on, and you will be able to enjoy everything as well.

If you want to add a different twist to this game, you could write erotica yourself, featuring you and your partner, and then act it out, step by step by step. Make sure that it is plenty steamy—make sure that it is a turn on and that it is also something that you can both enjoy.

Find a porn video that you both like... and reenact it

Now, porn is rarely actually good sex. There is sex that looks good, and there is sex that feels good, and the sex that is able to hit both of those points at the same time is exceedingly rare. However, you might get lucky and find it. Choose out some porn and watch it together, enacting everything that you see so that you can enjoy each and every moment of it as well. If you can do this regularly, you will find that you will totally spice up what you are doing, and you will drive your partner crazy.

Read erotica to each other

Find some erotica online and read it with each other. You can take turns reading it out loud with each other, getting used to the dirty words, and potentially even finding some stuff that you would enjoy trying out yourself if you happen to get lucky. Try out the moves that you read about in the erotica and see if it is actually as sexy to act out as it is to read about. Who knows, you might find your next favorite position this way! There are plenty of different websites online where you can find all sorts of great erotica, free of charge and without any strings attached, meaning you don't have to leave home or buy anything at all to do this.

Mix and match

You can also put several of these different challenges together to really up the ante on it all. If you want to have mind-blowing sex, you need to be willing to experiment and to make sure that ultimately, you enjoy what you are doing. It may be unconventional, but there is nothing wrong with that. It may involve copious amounts of dirty talk, but there is nothing wrong with that, either. It may involve all sorts of things or positions that you never thought you would do, but that's okay too. Sex is one of those things that is not, by any means, one size fits all. There are so many different options out there for you that you can do, and there are many things that some people swear by that would make other people blanch. So long as you and your partner are finding that it is hot, that is all that matters!

Conclusion

And with that, we have made it to the end of this book. Hopefully, you have read this book with your partner and took the time to really get to know what it is that you and your partner really want. It is important that if you are going to be intimate with someone, whether they are a one night stand, a long-term partner, or even your spouse, you want to make sure that you are communicating.

Dirty talk itself is just another form of communication, but it is one that must be preceded by other concepts as well. If you want to use dirty talk to turn your partner on, you want to make sure that you are always engaging in the right kinds of behaviors. You want to make sure that ultimately, you and your partner are on the right page with everything, and if you can be on the same page as each other, you can usually ensure that the sex that you will have will be mind-blowing. After all, nothing is better than fucking someone that is naturally going to follow your moves, pay attention to your particular desires, and make sure that you are happy. If you can do this, you will have plenty of success.

Before you dive right into dirty talking with your partner, then make sure that you communicate. Is it sexy to talk about boundaries? Not traditionally, but you are conveying your own emotions and that you care about the other person and their boundaries, which is highly erotic itself. Make sure that you and your partner are on the same page with everything that you do so that you will be able to control your enjoyment as well.

From there, all you have to do is get creative. When you know what each other's boundaries are, you can get to work, physically and mentally as well. You can send dirty messages to your partner. You can beg them to fuck you or to let you fuck them. You can encourage them to do things that you may normally have been too afraid to say. You can make sure that you are in complete and utter control over your sexual relationship, and if you can make that happen, you are going to find that your sex life will be better than ever. You can teach your partner to crave you more than anything else. You can teach your partner to want you constantly, or that you can turn him or her on in an instant just by knowing what they like to hear and how you can really tickle that fancy and get them going. All you need to do is make sure that when you are talking to your partner, you are spending the time to be erotic.

Remember, all you need to do is describe what is happening. Remember that there are three keys here: Say what you are going to do, what you are doing, and what you just did. If you can be descriptive like this, you don't even have to think much about the dirty talk that is happening. All you have to do is just that—

narrate what you are doing so that your partner will be even more turned on. Maybe you tell him, "I'm going to ride your hard cock." Then, you say, "Ooh, I love riding your hard cock." Later, when you are done, you can say, "I'm so glad I got to ride your cock." You are essentially just regurgitating out one sentiment in three different ways, but this descriptiveness is a great way to not only turn your partner on because you know that you are already saying things that are narrating actions that happen to turn your partner on.

You should also remember that expressing your desire is crucial as well, especially if you do it with commands. These are all keys to making sure that you can drive your partner wild, and if you can remember these point sand take them into your bedroom with you, you will find that you are highly successful with everything that you are doing. All you need to do is make sure that you are effective in what you are doing.

Thank you for taking the time to read through this book, and remember, dirty talk is a skill. Just like any other skill, it can be natural for some people, but for most, it is something that will take effort and practice. You must commit to what you are doing. You must make sure that you are taking the time to practice and that you are willing to deal with the trial and error. It may not always be the most fun, and it may be embarrassing sometimes, but if you can remember to keep on going, you can learn to say all sorts of things that will turn your partner on instantly so that you can have the time, or the fuck, of your life.

Finally, if you found that this book was beneficial in providing you with tips that will help you to properly master foreplay through dirty talk, or if you feel like the information and activities will help to spice up your sex life, please consider heading over to Amazon and leaving a review with your experience. It could help others find the information that they need to get it going on in bed too, and it would also be greatly appreciated! Your feedback is always well received and helps to ensure that future books are even better than the last ones. Thank you, once more, and good luck, with all your bedroom adventures! May your fucking be fun, and may your orgasms be mind-blowing!

Description

Do you want to spice up your sex life? Are you tired of a boring bedroom? Do you feel like something is missing in your relationship? If so, then keep reading...

Sometimes, you can feel like that spark, that passion that kept your bed burning with red-hot desire, is starting to fade. You can feel like your partner is losing interest, or worse—losing attraction for you. When the bedroom starts to feel dull, after all, how much fun can bedroom time actually be?

That is where dirty talk comes in. When you are able to bring dirty talk into the room and into your life, you can reignite that spark. You can get the juices flowing, the blood pumping, and the desire burning hotter than ever. All you have to do is learn how to use it. After all, there is a dramatic difference between asking someone to insert their genitalia into your genitalia repeatedly and forcefully versus saying something sexy and dirty enough to make even a porn star blush. If you know what you are doing, you can make your partner practically drool for you.

No matter if you are a man or a woman, or if your partner is a man or a woman, this book is for you—you can learn what to expect, how to talk to your partner to make him or her all hot and bothered and desperate to rip your clothes off of you. Whether you have never said a naughty word in your life or if you are already well versed in talking dirty but want to take it a step further, this book can help you.

Dirty talk is meant to be inherently sexual, highly erotic, and able to turn you and your partner on. Of course, this will vary from person to person—but you can make it work for you, no matter what your fetishes. Whether you want to be slapped across the face and choked, or you just want a little bit of excitement in your bedroom life, this book will teach you everything you need to know. In particular, you can expect to find:

- An understanding of what dirty talk is and why it is not inherently disrespectful—but it can be

- How to use dirty talk in your relationship in a way that is erotic and enjoyable for you and your partner, no matter what your boundaries are

- How to use dirty talk as a form of foreplay to keep your partner turned on and desperate for your body

- Insight into the mind of the man and his desires, as well as how you can speak to men to turn them on

- Information on how to understand women and what they want
- An introduction to sexting and everything that goes with it
- All sorts of things to NOT do in the bedroom
- *AND MORE*

With over 200 tips and tricks to use in your relationship, this book will teach you to be more of a turn on than anything else. All you have to do is start to implement the tools that you will be given in this book. Don't spend one more night in agony, wishing for a better time—scroll up and click on BUY NOW today!

www.ingramcontent.com/pod-product-compliance
Lightning Source LLC
Chambersburg PA
CBHW071516080526
44588CB00011B/1438